Praise

'Nature is the most valuable asset on Earth, yet for centuries we have priced it at zero. *Rewilding Wealth* makes the economic case for nature so compelling that ignoring it is no longer rational. This is the book that finally bridges conservation and capital.'

— Rob Gardner, CEO and Co-Founder, Rebalance Earth, and author of *Freedom: Earn it Keep it, Grow it*

'In *Rewilding Wealth,* Rich Stockade delivers a thought-provoking analysis of the potential for natural capital to move beyond the realms of conventional ESG funding, to become a fully fledged asset class with real value based on the benefits nature delivers society.

— George Eustice, Managing Director, Penbroath Ltd, and former Secretary of State for the Environment, Food and Rural Affairs

'*Rewilding Wealth* by Rich Stockdale is a punchy, polemical field report from the front line of the natural capital revolution – written by the man building Britain's first conservation-focused unicorn.'

— Ben Keene, Co-Founder, The Rebel Book Club, Raaise, and Good with AI

'This is the blueprint being written in real time. Simply incredible! A must-read if you want to stay on top of both landscape-wide nature regeneration and institutional-scale nature finance.'

— Elena Doms, Director of Europe, Oxygen Conservation

'Uplifting and optimistic, *Rewilding Wealth* is an antidote to fearmongering, built on aspiration for change led by private investment rather than funding from the public purse. This private–public debate forms a core part of the narrative. The book is brave in its remit, and I would urge everyone to absorb and act on the message. In the words of the author: the future is arriving faster than we thought.'

— David Hill, Founder, President, Foundation For Nature

'The themes in *Rewilding Wealth* serve as a salient roadmap for scaling natural capital to a profound degree. Rich has put his finger on the nerve of what has begun to emerge and still needs to coalesce for mass market adoption of nature-based solutions.'

— Tripp Wall, Founder and CEO, Pantheon PBC

'Most books about natural capital talk numbers. This one talks culture, courage, and the uncomfortable truths our sector needs to hear. Rich has written the playbook for treating conservation not as charity but as the most exciting asset class of our generation.'

— Cain Blythe, Founder and CEO, CreditNature and Ecosulis, and author of *The Fear Paradox*

'Rich Stockdale and the Oxygen Conservation team are blazing a trail in the development of natural capital markets. This is how we restore nature at scale, through the mobilisation of private capital and the realignment of incentives around land management. *Rewilding Wealth* tells a hugely important story for our time.'

— Ben Goldsmith, Chief Executive, Menhaden, and host of the *Rewilding the World* podcast

'We are at a critical point in history, with an unmissable opportunity to build the natural capital market and develop a more nature-connected economy. Turning private sector investment in the restoration of the natural environment into a commercial proposition is no small undertaking. In *Rewilding Wealth*, Rich communicates in a confident and honest way as he reflects on the challenges – and offers his fascinating perspective on how we can tackle those together.'

— Mark Clayton, CEO, Triodos Bank UK

'A characteristically energetic, highly personal and expansive reflection on the business of natural capital. *Rewilding Wealth* is jam-packed-full of bold ideas and perspectives that will continue to spark and fuel debate across the sector and beyond.'

— Alexa Culver, General Counsel, RSK Wilding

'One can sometimes find good books that point the way towards a better environmental future, and one can sometimes find books that are beautifully written elegies to nature. One does not usually find one that does both at the same time. *Rewilding Wealth* is that rare bird. Not only is it full of clear-headed, practical and financially savvy indication of what our society needs to do to build a better future, but it is beautifully written and engaging.'

— Ricardo Bayon, Partner and Co-founder, Encourage Capital, and Adjunct Professor, Brown University

'Rich Stockdale has crafted a book that feels both urgent and optimistic. It is unapologetically challenging, often uncomfortable, and consistently inspiring. What sets it apart is its extraordinary clarity of purpose: to professionalise conservation, to unlock natural capital at scale, and to prove that profit and ecological restoration are not opposing forces, but powerful allies when aligned with integrity.'

— James Farrell, Partner, Head of Rural Consultancy, Knight Frank

'*Rewilding Wealth* arrives at exactly the right moment, when the natural capital sector is moving from aspiration to centre stage, from pilot projects to asset class. This is not a book about saving nature in spite of markets; it's a blueprint for saving nature through them. Whether you come from finance, policy, or land management, *Rewilding Wealth* will challenge your assumptions, provoke your thinking, and ultimately energise you to move faster.'

— Eoin Murray, CIO, Rebalance Earth

'*Rewilding Wealth* challenges the reader to consider how each of us views the environment and our exploitation of the globe's natural capital. Driven by Rich's energy and data-led enthusiasm, Oxygen Conservation is looking to build the future for environmental investment.'

— Charles Ellis, BDO, Partner, London Audit

'*Rewilding Wealth* is an essential book. It is urgent, optimistic, and ambitious. This is not a conventional environmental treatise filled with statistics and despair. Instead, it is bold and original: a manifesto that talks of conservation as a high-performance, investable enterprise capable of delivering meaningful ecological restoration alongside genuine financial returns. Rich Stockdale is the Jimi Hendrix of conservation – he's redefining traditional approaches, technically exceptional, building influence in an unconventional way. He disrupts the norm, irritating the incumbents, and writes with real passion. Rich would be the last person to claim he's kickstarting a revolution alone – he frequently and generously namechecks his community of peers – but he's the one with the microphone and the amp. And if Rich succeeds, then I think we all will.'

— Ben Stansfield, Head of Natural Capital, Gowling WLG

'*Rewilding Wealth* is a bold and ambitious push to make natural capital tangible. Price it, or we won't value it – it's that simple. The sooner this clicks, the faster we can build a sustainable future.'

— Tommy Ricketts, CEO and Co-Founder, BeZero

'Rich has done something extraordinary in this book: he's given the environmental movement a language that finance can finally understand. For too long, we've watched nature degrade because its value simply didn't appear on any balance sheet. *Rewilding Wealth* changes that. Rich understands something fundamental: pricing nature isn't about commodifying it; it's about protecting it. This should be required reading for every financier, every policymaker, and every conservationist who wonders why we're losing the battle. We now have the tools to build a financial system that rewards restoration rather than destruction. Rich has given us the roadmap.'

— James Byrne, Head of Nature Markets, Plantlife

'Always thought-provoking, often controversial; in this collection of essays Rich Stockdale sets out his thoughts on nature, capital, and change. From considering how to reshape the cultural terrain in which conservation is understood and valued to articulating why we need to embrace the unorthodox, Stockdale calls for nothing less than a paradigm shift in how we engage with nature markets. He believes that only by changing our mindset will it be possible to un-tap the "trillion-dollar opportunity hidden in plain sight" that is natural capital.'

— Andrew Hicks, CEO, BNGx

'For those of us that believe in nature as the most exciting and important new infrastructure asset class to have emerged in years, we have a dilemma: how do we convey the urgency and the value of investment at scale in this sector? *Rewilding Wealth* expertly sets out what is required. Rich's passion is genuine and immediate, and the underlying argument is watertight: you cannot shame people into loving nature, but by bringing people together, we can make protecting it as profitable, predictable and safe an investment as any.'

— Nath Curtis, Partner, Jones Day

'Our society and economy fundamentally and absolutely depend on the Earth system which provides essentials such as food, water, energy and raw materials. But our current economic model risks pushing that system into a much less habitable state, threatening future prosperity and life on Earth. Solving for how to mainstream nature into finance is beyond critical. This book and the Oxygen Conservation journey provide a beacon, illuminating the way forwards for how this can work in practice – a hugely valuable contribution.'

— Sandy Trust, Planetary Solvency Lead, IFOA

'What I love about this book is its ambition. It clearly sets out the investment case and demonstrates a commercial, scalable opportunity for investors.'

— Andy Creak, CEO, Kana Earth

'Here's to the crazy ones. The misfits. The rebels. The troublemakers. The round pegs in the square holes. The ones who see things differently. They're not fond of rules. And they have no respect for the status quo. You can quote them, disagree with them, glorify or vilify them. About the only thing you can't do is ignore them – because they change things. This book is one of them. Be stimulated and enjoy.'

— James Alexander MBE, former Chair, Finance Earth

'*Rewilding Wealth* is a provocative and compelling vision for how we can align investment, talent, and purpose to restore nature at scale. This book pushes the sector to think bigger – and faster – about what's possible.'

— Crawford Mackay, Partner, Galbraith

'*Rewilding Wealth* captures something that many people in the natural capital sector feel but rarely articulate so clearly: that we are living through the early chapters of a profound economic and cultural shift in how nature is valued. The combination of storytelling, commercial realism, and ecological ambition running through the book mirrors the approach Oxygen has taken in practice: building a business that demonstrates conservation can scale when it is treated with the same rigour, creativity, and ambition as any other major industry.'

— Will Foulkes, CEO and Co-Founder, Stabiliti

'Rich and Oxygen Conservation are trailblazers. This book is a wonderful map of how they do it. A must-read for anyone serious about nature restoration at scale. I loved it.'

— Hector Hughes, Co-Founder and CEO, Unplugged

'Filled with genuinely inspiring and operationally helpful stories, *Rewilding Wealth* is the perfect book for anyone interested in how we can sustainably address the decline in natural habitats in the UK.'

— Piers Clark, Founder, Isle Group Ltd.

REWILDING WEALTH

FROM EXTRACTIVE CAPITALISM TO REGENERATIVE RETURNS

DR RICH STOCKDALE

First published in Great Britain in 2026
by Rethink Press (www.rethinkpress.com)

Disclaimer

This book is written for general informational and educational purposes only. It does not constitute any form of advice, recommendation, representation, endorsement, arrangement, financial promotion, or invitation to invest, and is not intended to be relied upon by users in making (or refraining from making) any specific investment or other decisions. No responsibility for any loss or damage arising from reliance on the content will be accepted. All opinions expressed are those of the author in his personal capacity. References to third-party organisations, institutions and individuals are made for contextual purposes only and do not imply endorsement of the author's views.

Contents

Foreword

For centuries, the global economic system has placed economic values on natural capital, but we are witnessing a fundamental shift in how valuations are reached and the framework within which decisions are taken. Markets increasingly view nature as infrastructure. The parallels are palpable; both nature and infrastructure must be developed and maintained with careful investment to mitigate the risk of degradation.

When I led the Advisory Group on Economic Recovery in 2020, one of our most important conclusions was the absolute need to view natural capital as being as important as financial capital, human capital, and social capital. It is only by having an unequivocal view that nature must not be considered expendable that nature is recognised as having value.

This is the kernel of purpose of Oxygen Conservation. It's why I was honoured to become Chairman and work with the Board to support an outstanding team pursuing groundbreaking initiatives. Public funding alone is very unlikely to be enough to set the right agenda or provide the resources to drive that agenda. It is an ineluctable reality that only by drawing private capital will the urgency be met with commensurate discipline and investment. One hopes that public–private partnerships will flourish in this landscape. A strong foundation of education and awareness is essential. And this must include the political class and policy makers.

Predictably, financial markets are traversing the knowledge curve with real momentum, and general public awareness will grow. But policy and regulation can be catalysts or obstacles. Let's be persuasive in making the case that a progressive, enabling framework is essential. Natural capital must be integrated into financial systems. Investors and businesses will be incentivised by the formality of evidencing the economic markets for natural capital, such as carbon credits and biodiversity credits. That will, in turn, lubricate engagement with communities and those involved in key decision-making processes. This will extend across sectors such as agriculture, forestry, fisheries, and many others.

As with all pursuits in the twenty-first century, collection and analysis of data will be key to efficiency and effectiveness delivering sustainable excellence. Natural capital is now recognised as an asset. That staging post is behind us.

At Oxygen Conservation, we are not at the beginning of the journey, but the pace of change is about to accelerate, and we are determined to be prepared and ready to contribute to projects that lie at the heart of the wellbeing of the planet and its people. In the words of Hellen Keller, 'Optimism is the faith that leads to achievement. Nothing can be done without hope and confidence.' We face challenges and opportunities with realistic optimism.

Benny Higgins
Chairman, Oxygen Conservation

Introduction: Reading Between The Wild Lines

First, let's manage some expectations: if you're seeking straightforward instructions, bullet points, or academic text, this is not what you're going to find in my writing. My words are not meant to serve as a set of explicit directions or essays. Instead, I take great pleasure in engaging with language in all its complexity, exploring its contradictions, nuances, and possibilities. Language isn't just a means of communication; it's an opportunity for creative expression and a way of seeing and shaping the world, especially when the world we're working in is changing faster than ever before.

This is especially true when we're writing about nature, capital, and change. We are not just describing the landscape; we are shaping the cultural terrain in which conservation is understood and valued.

Complexity isn't a flaw in this system; it's a feature.

Ambiguity as an asset

I write from a place that deliberately tries to balance clarity and complexity. This is intentional. It's within these challenging spaces that meaningful reflection and critical thinking happen. Our company, Oxygen Conservation, frequently confronts complex issues full of contradictions and compromises, and my writing aims to capture the realities my team and I explore every day. I encourage you to engage with and enjoy these tensions, using them to stimulate thought, provoke debate, and inspire fresh ideas.

Each of these ambiguities is an invitation to look closer, think harder, and ask different questions. Writing about real-world systems that impact climate, biodiversity, and economics means embracing uncertainty and evolution. That's where genuine insight lives, or at least emerges from occasionally. When we explore natural capital, we're also exploring the intersections of our relationship with the environment, economics, morality, and psychology.

Please don't hope to find simplicity in my writing; I'm not prepared to sacrifice everything that simplicity demands. Instead, I aspire to compel you to pause, reflect, and appreciate the potential of language. I want my words to linger, not just inform. In a world saturated with content, truly thoughtful writing has become a rare gift. When done well, it can move you emotionally and intellectually, and that's exactly what I aspire to do.

Our language therefore needs to do much more than just describe. We ask our words to do the heavy lifting, to bear the full weight of ideas that stretch across systems and values.

Intentionally incomplete

Do not expect easy conclusions, these can be both boring and unnecessary, or neatly packaged summaries from my work. At Oxygen Conservation, we view our written material as part of an ongoing conversation rather than a final word. We share real-world stories and insights found in our lived experiences, seen in successes and setbacks, or crafted through continual adjustments. Think of this book as dialogue, not doctrine. Each section is an idea at a point in time, an unfinished sentence that only you, the reader, can complete. We're building knowledge iteratively, transparently, and collectively.

Adapting to evolution

Through writing, we at Oxygen Conservation document and explore significant shifts within the rapidly evolving fields of natural capital, asset management, rewilding, and sustainability. As this sector evolves, our writing helps us adapt, communicate more effectively, and process the emotional highs and lows that come with leading change in uncertain territory. Writing gives us space to reflect, to exhale, and to turn frustration or fear into something constructive: a line of thought, a lesson learned, or even just the relief of having named something difficult out loud.

In this way, writing becomes a shared act of emotional resilience. It helps us not only make sense of what we're feeling, but also connect with others in the sector who may be feeling the same. In doing so, we begin to build something powerful, not just an organisation or a movement, but a community. One not tied to geography, but bound by a shared optimism, a refusal to be paralysed by complexity, and the conviction that doing something, anything, matters. That trying counts. That hope is found in action. This writing is not just how we keep track of our journey, it's how we cope with it.

Embedded within this book are references, acknowledgments, and tributes to important people, special moments, and significant places. These nuanced details are never accidental, they're placed with intention and designed to be hidden in plain sight. Not all words, phrases, or sentences are what they first appear to be. Everything is there for a reason. I, and the team at Oxygen Conservation, don't do anything 'just because'.

Of course, not everything will land with every reader. That's the point. You might catch a phrase and wonder if there's more to it. There likely is, but if a deeper meaning escapes you this time, don't worry. Perhaps the next passage of text is the one is for you.

Learning out loud

As you engage with this book, please remember I am learning too. My writing captures the insights and reflections from ongoing experiences, conversations, and challenges. Rather than definitive answers, I often present open-ended questions, inviting further thought and exploration. I acknowledge my flaws and limitations openly, knowing that genuine discovery and growth occur precisely through uncomfortableness, vulnerability, humility, and honesty.

At Oxygen Conservation, this is our process of learning out loud. We test ideas in public. We welcome disagreement, not because we always want to win arguments (although sometimes we do), but because we want to understand. This transparency, something no longer radical to us, is a cornerstone of how we think and how we hope others do too.

This book is intended to invite your active, passionate participation. Please share your perspectives, especially those that challenge mine, as they enrich the collective understanding. Your insights, contributions, and questions are crucial in building a vibrant community committed to shaping a sustainable future.

Think of yourself not just as a reader, but as a collaborator. What you gain from this book, what you add to it, question about it, or challenge in it, helps shape the future of the natural capital economy.

Welcome to the thoughtfully complex, audaciously ambitious, relentlessly optimistic, and continually chaotic world of Oxygen Conservation.

ONE

The Origins Of Obsession

What We Don't Price, We Don't Value

Written October 2024

For decades, environmental advocates have championed the idea of pricing carbon, arguing that attaching a clear financial cost to emitting carbon dioxide and other greenhouse gases from burning fossil fuels is essential. This would transform what have been cost- and consequence-free acts of pollution into financially accountable ones.

Yet, despite its critical importance, carbon pricing has previously struggled to establish itself in the financial mainstream. The patchwork of inconsistent policies from nation to nation has led to a fragmented and often ineffective system. Now, as we face environmental and social oblivion, the need to use price to value and protect our indispensable natural assets has never been more paramount.

The climate crisis is accelerating, with record-breaking temperatures, more extreme weather events, more floods (and droughts), and fires becoming more frequent and severe. The social costs, including displacement, health issues, and economic losses, are mounting. This urgency underscores the need to recognise and account for the environmental costs of fossil fuel consumption through robust carbon pricing mechanisms.

The role of carbon markets

Carbon markets do not privatise or exonerate pollution or polluters. They are simply accounting systems, like any other, that assign value where the lack of it has led to the obscene denigration of that which we have considered ours to use freely, at no cost. By failing to assign value to our natural environment, we have allowed for its wilful, unchecked degradation and destruction.

The basic premise of carbon markets is straightforward: they aim to reduce fossil fuel consumption and utilise carbon credits to offset emissions that cannot be eliminated. This system recognises that intangible yet indispensable natural assets have been taken financially for granted, and thus essentially laid to waste. Effective carbon markets ensure that the true cost of environmental damage is reflected in the price of goods and services, incentivising businesses to innovate, adapt, and reduce their carbon footprints.

We have become used to a take-what-you-can approach. The result? Pollution, degradation, climate change, and a false security that nature's services will never cease to function, no matter how exploitative and abusive we all are.

To reverse this process and better value the atmosphere, carbon markets put a price on using increasingly rare space for greenhouse gas pollution. The more space you occupy with pollutants, in theory, the more you pay, so the incentive develops to take up less space (ie, pollute less).

We all now recognise and accept that we must pay for the use of space, be it for our possessions (banks and storage facilities), our vehicles (car parks and garages), our waste (recycling and disposal bins), or ourselves (homes and hotels). Yet we still resist applying this same principle to the way we use our most precious space, the atmosphere.

Shortcomings of financial systems

Traditional financial systems have fallen far short of protecting the planet. Capitalism, as it currently stands, prioritises short-term exploitation and gain over long-term sustainability, and needs to change its priorities to avoid catastrophic environmental and social detriment. The inherent problem lies in the failure to account for the true value of natural assets. Without a financial framework that recognises the worth of clean air, water, and biodiversity, these resources are depleted without regard for the days to come.

Capitalism needs to evolve to prioritise long-term environmental and social wellbeing over short-term profits. This requires a fundamental shift in how we all define success and measure economic progress. By incorporating carbon pricing and other environmental considerations into our financial systems, we can create a model of capitalism that supports truly sustainable development. This new model would emphasise metrics like social return on investment (SROI) and alignment with the United Nations Sustainable Development Goals (UN-SDGs), uniting business performance with broader societal aims.

Pricing carbon and other natural capital assets makes them visible in financial terms. This visibility is crucial for illuminating both the value of saving and protecting these assets and the cost of losing them. As we face expanding environmental and social risks, there is a paramount need to use price to value and shield the assets that invisibly, for the most part, underpin our wellbeing. When these assets have notable financial value, protecting them becomes a logical and compelling proposition for businesses and policymakers alike.

By quantifying the economic benefits of preserving ecosystems, such as the role woodlands play in carbon sequestration or the importance of wetlands in flood mitigation, we can create stronger incentives for conservation. This economic visibility helps align private and public interests and investments in maintaining and restoring natural resources.

The evolution of value in the global economy

The global economy is evolving from valuing traditional tangible goods, such as manufactured products, to placing greater importance on intangible assets. Brands, apps, intellectual property, service industries, and advanced research and development are now seen as the pillars of modern economic value. This transformation invites a rethinking of what underpins money as legal tender in a world where value is less about physical goods and more about ideas, innovation, and digital presence.

The rise of the digital economy illustrates how non-physical assets can drive substantial value creation. This paradigm shift provides a framework for integrating environmental assets into financial markets, recognising their essential role in supporting economic stability and regenerative growth.

The case for environmental assets as financial instruments

The emergence of alternative ideas about what backs up money as legal tender (think digital and cryptocurrencies) is an important consideration, reflecting a broader trend towards recognising the intrinsic value of sustainability. If transactions of once-esoteric homemade digital currencies are credible and acceptable, why not biodiversity units, nature credits, or carbon credits resting on the underlying value of lasting environmental health? Carbon credits can fund large-scale woodland creation schemes; biodiversity net gain (BNG) credits can be catalysts for habitat restoration and creation. By establishing these instruments as credible financial assets, we can drive investment towards sustainable practices and technologies.

Innovation and technology will play a crucial role in this transition. Digital platforms can enhance the transparency and efficiency of carbon markets, making it easier for businesses and individuals to participate. Blockchain technology, for example, can provide secure and transparent tracking of carbon credits, ensuring that emission reductions are verifiable and preventing fraud. Similarly, advancements in AI and data analytics can optimise regenerative land management and enhance the effectiveness of remote data acquisition and monitoring habitat creation and restoration.

Education and public awareness

Educating the public about the importance of carbon pricing and environmental protection is essential. When people understand the financial and ecological benefits of sustainable practices, they are more likely to support policies and initiatives that promote these goals.

Public awareness campaigns, educational programmes, and transparent communication from policymakers can help build the necessary support for carbon pricing. Engaging communities through participatory approaches can also foster a deeper connection to environmental issues, driving grassroots support for sustainable policies.

The urgency of pricing carbon cannot be overstated. As we face unprecedented environmental and social challenges, it is imperative that we recognise the true value of our natural assets. By integrating carbon pricing into the financial mainstream, we can create a more sustainable and equitable economy that prioritises the wellbeing of both people and the planet.

This transition requires international cooperation, innovative thinking, and a commitment to redefining value in a way that ensures a prosperous future for all. Embracing this change will not only protect our environment, but also promote social equity and economic resilience.

The above piece was heavily influenced by the work and writing of Paula DiPerna in her book *Pricing the Priceless: The financial transformation to value the planet, solve the climate crisis, and protect our most precious assets* (2023). I continue to recommend the book as a must-read for those interested in the intersection of financial systems and the natural world.

On reflection

If we don't price nature, we permit its destruction. This reminds us that until clean air, thriving ecosystems, and stable climates are visible on balance sheets, they will remain invisible in boardrooms. Carbon pricing isn't a tax, it's a truth-teller. It's how we make the invisible visible, and the priceless protectable.

In the wonderful wise words of Charlie Munger, 'Show me the incentive and I will show you the outcome' (Miltimore, 2023).

Pinstripes to Patagonia: The Cultural Uprising Rewriting Conservation

Written May 2025

The conservation sector, for all its good intentions, has often wrapped itself in the language of science and policy so tightly that few outside the echo chamber could hear what mattered most. For decades, it whispered noble intentions through dense reports and dusty conference halls, failing to ignite the imagination of the very people it needed to galvanise.

Finally, gloriously, that's changing.

We are witnessing a radical shift in how nature, climate, and conservation are being communicated. This change is not ornamental; it is structural. It marks a new age where data meets drama, and where natural capital is not only measured, but felt. In this seismic transformation, communication isn't a side-show, it's the main event.

Storytelling has stepped out from the margins to take its rightful place at the centre of environmental strategy, investment, and impact. It's giving the natural capital sector something it's long needed: an edge.

At the heart of this seismic transformation is communication. This isn't merely about clearer messaging or more accessible language, although both matter deeply. Rather, it's a profound cultural shift towards embracing storytelling, emotion, authenticity, and direct engagement. It's about finishing stories – turning scientific data points into relatable narratives with clear beginnings, compelling middles, and resonant conclusions. Stories matter because they capture hearts, inspire action, and evoke empathy far more powerfully than any spreadsheet or PowerPoint presentation ever could. Of course, these are necessary and important, but not without the stories to bring them to life.

Consider for a moment the powerful resonance of storytelling in other fields. Patagonia didn't become a legendary outdoor apparel company simply by manufacturing durable jackets. Its power and appeal lie in the deeply emotional, authentic, sometimes controversial stories its people tell, boldly embracing activism, environmental advocacy, and human experiences.

Similarly, Finisterre, a brand deeply rooted, just like Oxygen Conservation, in the South West of the UK, evokes images of cold-water surfing and adventure, and has mastered a narrative approach, successfully weaving personal tales of hardship, triumph, and environmental stewardship seamlessly into its brand identity. These companies don't just market products; they engage people in collective journeys, creating emotional bonds that are profoundly powerful and lasting.

Contrast these rich, textured narratives with the traditional flat monochromatic of conservation: muddy browns, muted greens, quiet understatement. Such dreariness does little to spark imagination or rally action. Yet recently, the conservation sector has begun incorporating dazzling shades and vibrant stories, boldly leveraging Technicolor creativity alongside more understated narratives. Both have their roles; together they captivate far more effectively than their washed-out predecessors. When we tell stories of nature conservation today, we blend stunning visuals, emotional honesty, and experiential depth.

The influx of talented creative communicators into conservation is not merely refreshing, it's transformative. Photographers, videographers, podcasters, producers, authors, and orators are now entering a space previously restricted to ecologists and academics.

Many of these dynamic voices belong to women and diverse young people, awakening the entire sector. The impact of their fresh perspectives cannot be overstated. They're injecting adventure, humour, fun, and genuine human emotion into a space too long reserved for dry academic discourses and bureaucratic jargon. Imagine the shift from a dreary conference slideshow detailing amphibian population declines to an emotionally gripping short film featuring firsthand experiences of conservationists braving harsh terrains and challenging hurdles to restore habitats.

Such stories create connections, build communities, not purely geographically, and foster a collective sense of responsibility and passion. Moreover, these creative communicators are masters at leveraging digital platforms. Social media, YouTube, podcasts, and immersive websites are their canvases. They transform complex science into digestible, compelling narratives accessible to everyone, dismantling barriers that once made conservation feel distant and irrelevant to many people.

Suddenly, conservation isn't academic, it's personal, vibrant, relatable, and inspiring. It's critical to recognise that this creative awakening is not merely cosmetic or superficial; it's strategically vital. Nature conservation and the burgeoning field of natural capital investment thrive on public engagement and investor confidence. Both depend heavily on clear, compelling storytelling that vividly communicates purpose, progress, and potential. Investors increasingly seek impactful, meaningful ventures. Emotional narratives, grounded in rigorous science but delivered with creativity and passion, convince them far more effectively than dry statistical reports ever could.

Notably, the changing demographics of communicators are helping reshape the entire sector's culture. The visible presence and influence of younger voices, diverse backgrounds, and particularly talented women are reshaping not just how conservation is communicated, but how it's perceived, prioritised, and funded. For a sector historically dominated by elderly white men, a category I reluctantly find myself aging into faster than I'd prefer, this shift is profound and energising.

Ultimately, the integration of diverse, creative communication into conservation heralds a brighter future. It transforms environmental advocacy into a vibrant cultural force, an engaging narrative accessible to millions, not just the enlightened few. It moves the conversation from exclusive circles of specialists to inclusive dialogues that inspire action across communities, ages, and backgrounds. We're entering a thrilling era in conservation, an era of bold storytelling, emotional honesty, and vibrant creativity.

It's a shift from pinstriped suits to Patagonia's captivating adventures, from rigid conference halls to immersive escapes and interactive digital platforms, and I couldn't be more excited. Conservation isn't just becoming more inclusive and appealing; it's becoming irresistibly compelling. The narrative of nature's future is being rewritten, and it promises to captivate all of us.

Welcome to the new language of nature.

On reflection

At its core, what we're doing for natural capital at Oxygen Conservation is embarrassingly simple to explain and incredibly hard to execute. We are making natural capital culturally cool. Not polite, not worthy, not quietly important, but genuinely exciting in the same way great brands, athletes, and stories are exciting.

That means borrowing from the ambition of Blackstone, the energy of Red Bull, and the authenticity of Patagonia. We will let others decide whether we're succeeding, but I'm certain of one thing: conservation gets a lot more interesting when we stop whispering about nature decline and start telling stories that make people feel something.

Decoding Nature: We Are All Creating the New Language of Natural Capital

Written January 2025

The natural capital revolution is happening, a transformative shift that offers an unparalleled opportunity to reshape not only the economy, but the very language we use to describe our relationship with the natural world. To grasp the magnitude of this change, imagine trying to explain the internet in the 1980s, before Google, streaming services, and iPhones existed. The confusion surrounding natural capital today is strikingly similar, but this concept is poised to become as integral to our lives as the technology that powers our daily routines.

In the next decade, as systems to recognise nature as a tangible asset evolve, so too will our vocabulary. Yet, the language of natural capital today remains mired in academic jargon, acronyms, and technical terms that are not only daunting, but disengaging. If we can't all connect with these ideas, how can we be expected to care or act? This is a critical gap, and closing it is essential if we are to ensure that nature's value is understood and protected by all.

Take a lesson from the tech world: new terms seamlessly integrate into our daily lives as the technology matures. We no longer 'search the internet'; we 'Google'. We don't 'watch videos online'; we 'stream' them. This effortless transition will be mirrored in the world of natural capital. One day, we may not speak of 'carbon offsets' in cumbersome technical jargon, but in simple, universally understood terms that resonate. Just as 'posting' has come to represent sharing something on social media, the future of natural capital will bring its own streamlined terminology that will enter our language.

However, there's a significant challenge: much of what we're discussing in terms of natural capital, carbon, emissions, biodiversity, remains invisible to the naked eye. We cannot easily see the carbon we emit or the biodiversity being lost. Moreover, environmental damage often unfolds over long, abstract timelines, which makes it harder for people to grasp the urgency of the issue.

These factors make our mission even more crucial: we need to simplify, to make natural capital tangible and emotionally resonant, bringing these abstract forces into everyday understanding. We need more wonderful communicators, marketers, and psychologists working in the environment sector, so that even the term 'environment sector' is no longer meaningful because it's part of everything we do.

Each conversation we have today is an opportunity to shape this emerging language, an opportunity to practise what and how we communicate about natural capital. Just as terms like 'carbon footprint' have entered the mainstream discourse, we now have the chance to shape how the world talks about and values natural capital. The way we communicate these concepts today will influence how they are perceived and acted upon tomorrow.

Language does more than reflect reality, it actively constructs it. As we move towards a future where nature's value is integrated into our economic systems as clearly as stock prices or property values, we must recognise that language is one of our most powerful tools. By crafting a shared vocabulary, we are not only describing an economy where nature is a vital asset, but also building the foundation for its long-term stewardship.

As natural capital gains prominence in global financial markets, the urgency to make this shift in perception, and language, becomes ever more pressing. The challenge is not just to protect our natural resources, but to fundamentally redefine how society values them. The words we choose will not merely reflect this new reality, they will help create it.

The real question is: how will you speak about it? Will you contribute to the movement that reframes our understanding of nature's worth, ensuring it holds its rightful place in our economic future? The opportunity to be a part of this linguistic and environmental revolution is here now, so let's choose our words wisely, because they will shape the world we will live in, or won't.

Thanks go to Oxygen Conservation's Adam Franks for inspiring this article by always asking the challenging questions and seeking to understand not just the *what,* but always the *why* and *how.*

On reflection

'Decoding Nature' wasn't really intended to just be about language. I hoped it would inspire a great recognition that we're in the early chapters of a story that doesn't yet have the right words. Perhaps more importantly, it's an open invitation to help write them.

The idea that we're all co-creating the new language of natural capital feels more relevant now than ever before. As markets scramble to understand the myriad acronyms, as policy fails to catch up to practice, and as more people begin to ask questions, the need for clarity isn't just academic, it's existential.

Language doesn't follow change. It drives it.

Natural capital is no longer a niche concept, whispered in policy meetings or locked away in PDFs only economists read. It's surfacing in boardrooms, schools, and even dinner table conversations, and just like during the early days of the internet, we're fumbling for the right metaphors. We're somewhere between protocol and poetry.

What we need now are not just better definitions, but better storytellers. People who can translate complexity into connection. People who can make carbon legible, biodiversity visible, and nature's value felt.

The power of this piece lies in its gentle provocation: every time we speak about natural capital, we're either reinforcing a barrier or building a bridge. The way we describe, share, joke about, post, pitch, and explain this concept will shape how it lands.

In a world where 'stream' once meant a trickle of water and now means media content, who's to say what 'rewilding' or 'nature positive' might come to mean a decade from now? Language evolves as fast as our courage to shape it.

Let's choose our words wisely.

Embracing the Unorthodox

Written October 2024

In the emerging and evolving natural capital economy, increasingly defined by urgency and fast-paced change, a key principle is clear: the more orthodox players there are, the bigger the advantage in being unorthodox. This insight, drawn from both sports and economics, offers a valuable perspective. As we face the complexities of integrating ecological value into the global economy, unconventional approaches are needed to unlock distinct advantages.

In professional sports, the relationship between unorthodoxy and innovation is stark. The more players stick to the conventional, the more space there is for an unorthodox player to change the game. The cricket revolution brought about by T20 serves as a fitting analogy here, teams and players willing to adapt and innovate (and often face criticism and ridicule for so doing) outpaced those who were content with traditional play. The natural capital economy, like any dynamic arena, requires us to constantly assess where innovation can bring a competitive edge, in this case, in the battle against climate change and biodiversity loss.

Orthodoxy, in this context, is not without merit. The rigour, stability, and predictability of traditional approaches create a foundation that is often necessary, especially in domains like conservation. These tried-and-true methods provide a sense of continuity, allowing projects to be understood, funded, and executed based on established frameworks. The challenge with orthodoxy lies in its inability to react swiftly to changing dynamics, particularly when the stakes are as high as they are in today's environmental and economic landscape.

The advantage of embracing the extraordinary lies in the willingness to take risks and defy established norms when the pace accelerates, and it needs to accelerate more. In the natural capital economy, this means moving beyond traditional conservation metrics and employing new tools to quantify and communicate the value of ecosystems, whether through biodiversity credits, carbon markets, or advanced technology. It requires recognising that sometimes the most impactful strategy is not to mimic the past, but to create a new playbook altogether.

Unorthodoxy at Oxygen Conservation

The interplay between orthodoxy and the unorthodox in natural capital is a balance, and there is room on the team for both approaches. The strength of adhering to orthodoxy lies in its ability to anchor practices in tested methodologies (like public sector bodies or charitable trusts), while its weakness is the risk of being left behind as new approaches emerge. Conversely, the power of the extraordinary lies in its capacity to reshape the field (with so many incredible new businesses entering the natural capital economy), with its weakness being the risk inherent in breaking away from the predictable, the certainty of attack and criticism, and the pressure of being an early mover in a field.

Professionals who bring an unorthodox approach to the natural capital sector can redefine the rules of engagement. For example, we at Oxygen Conservation resisted local pressure to maintain traditional land-use practices and instead focused on restoring native woodland and improving the temperate rainforest. This bold step away from the status-quo, despite opposition, exemplifies how innovation and risk-taking can lead to transformative environmental success.

Consider the application of creative destruction in conservation. At Oxygen Conservation, we've moved beyond conventional land management by removing sheep farming and reintroducing natural processes, embracing the idea of minimising overgrazing by reducing livestock numbers. This decision challenges long-held agricultural practices, but allows ecosystems to recover.

In addition to rewilding, we've taken an unorthodox stance on public access to private lands. While many landowners close off their estates to the public, we actively encourage community engagement and connection with nature. That doesn't mean we're immune from people who think it's still not accessible enough. By making the natural world more accessible through our ecotourism offerings, we foster a deeper societal commitment to conservation, even though it introduces complexity to our conservation goals.

Equally important is how we communicate our work. Radical transparency has been a cornerstone of our success. We embrace a storytelling approach that openly shares the successes and struggles of our projects, this was one of the major reasons for starting the *Shoot Room Sessions* podcast. This transparency builds trust and accountability, something that is rarely prioritised in the broader conservation sector.

Perhaps our most unorthodox move is our strategic focus on private equity as the best vehicle for Scaling Conservation. While the public and charitable sectors are often slow-moving and constrained by bureaucracy, private equity allows us to be agile and innovative. This approach, historically uncommon in conservation, although that is now changing, has allowed us to scale our impact rapidly and pursue large-scale rewilding and nature restoration projects.

Furthermore, we've pushed for the professionalisation of the environment sector. Instead of relying on volunteers and hobbyists, we've created structured aspirational career paths, helping attract the next generation of skilled professionals to this vital field. By elevating conservation roles to professional paid careers, we are transforming how the environment sector is perceived, making it as competitive and dynamic as finance or tech. This means we are able to attract exceptional candidates who are driven by a passion to save the world and have the skills and experience to actually do it.

It's time to embrace the unorthodox

In the rapidly evolving natural capital economy, the speed of play, akin to high-level sports, demands agility. The more environmental challenges grow in urgency, the greater the need for professionals capable of thinking and acting beyond established paradigms, those ready to embrace the extraordinary when the circumstances call for it. I'm incredibly fortunate to work with so many of these people.

The game has indeed changed, and the advantage lies with those willing to play a different game entirely.

The insights in this article draw heavily from Tim Wigmore's brilliant work in *Cricket 2.0* (2019) and *Crickonomics* (2023), where he masterfully chronicles the evolution of T20 cricket and how every facet of the game has transformed from its Test origins. His exploration of how a sport can adapt, innovate, and reconfigure itself in response to new pressures and demands served as a powerful inspiration. Thank you, Tim.

On reflection

In sport and life, there are rare talents you simply can't take your eyes off. They see things differently. They bend time, manipulate space, and make the impossible look inevitable. Footballer Lionel Messi weaving through six defenders. Tennis genius Roger Federer feathering a backhand. Cricketer Ben Stokes reverse-sweeping. It's not just skill, it's imagination, instinct, and a total disregard for convention, but not in an arrogant or dismissive way. It simply doesn't occur to these people to play anyone else's game.

Through the pages of this book, you'll meet the environmental equivalents of those generational talents. They're not just unorthodox. They are beautifully, deliberately, joyfully different.

That's exactly what it feels like working at Oxygen Conservation. We've got biodiversity rebels who make spreadsheets sing. Estate managers who talk about rewilding with the same precision as a surgeon and the same heart as a poet. Storytellers who've turned radical transparency into a playful expressionist art form. Environmentalists who disagree with the red tape and go over and above its requirements anyway.

From iconic temperate rainforests in Devon to rewilding wilderness in the highlands of Scotland, from the wonderful Welsh coast to the forever flatland of Norfolk, this isn't conservation as usual; it's reinvention. In true Oxygen Conservation style, we don't just make space for the unorthodox. We attract it. We nurture it. We bet on it.

This book, like every estate we manage, is full of misfits, crazy ones, rebels, and geniuses. Whether you're reading this on a hilltop, just about to go into the boardroom, or somewhere in between, know this: the future belongs to those willing to play a different game, and we're just getting started.

Pattern Breaking for the Planet

Written April 2025

Over the last few years, the world has undergone a series of deep, often disruptive shifts, changes that would go on to form the foundations of Oxygen Conservation. To begin with, we didn't have a name for them. We just had a sense that the rules were evolving, the ground was moving, and we had a once-in-a-generation opportunity to build something better.

Then we read *Pattern Breakers* by Mike Maples and Peter Ziebelman (2024). Suddenly, we had the frameworks and the language we'd been missing. These weren't just changes. These were **inflection points**.

Inflection points, as Maples and Ziebelman define them, are powerful forces of change that, when recognised and acted on, unlock transformative opportunity. They're not soft trends or slow drifts, they're tectonic shifts that redefine what's possible.

That's exactly what we set out to do.

Ten inflection points that shaped Oxygen Conservation

Here's a look at the ten inflection points that shaped the foundation of Oxygen Conservation. Some we anticipated. Some we discovered along the way. Others we worked hard to create.

All of them formed the opportunity to Scale Conservation and reimagine our relationship with nature, land, and the economy.

1. Climate crisis becomes a boardroom reality

Global shift: Climate risk is now financial risk. Wildfires, droughts, and floods are disrupting every industry and supply chain.

OC's response: We're not a sustainability bolt-on, we *are* the strategy. Our landscapes sequester carbon, absorb floodwaters, and build climate resilience. We don't wait for catastrophe. We engineer resilience into the land, locking in long-term value and impact.

2. Nature enters the market

Global shift: Natural capital – carbon, biodiversity, water – is now a priced asset. Ecosystems have entered the balance sheet.

OC's response: We didn't wait for the rules; we helped shape them. From literally sketching the curve for the future price of premium carbon credits to pioneering conservation-led biodiversity units, we've turned nature into traceable, transparent value. Restoring ecosystems and generating returns are no longer opposites, they're intertwined.

3. The agricultural subsidy collapse

Global shift: Brexit and UK policy reforms have rocked the agricultural sector. The subsidy system is crumbling and generational security is vanishing.

OC's response: We're building what comes next, a new framework for rural land ownership and management. One that blends natural capital, renewable energy, ecotourism, regenerative agriculture, and strategic land stewardship. This is rural reinvention with purpose and profit.

4. The rural renaissance

Global shift: Post-pandemic, people began leaving cities in search of space, meaning, and community. Rural is no longer remote, it's relevant.

OC's response: Our estates are not just for wildlife, they're for people too. From green jobs and rural housing to immersive ecotourism and wild swimming, we're rewilding more than land, we're rewilding lives.

5. Energy + ecology

Global shift: The race to net zero is accelerating demand for renewable-ready land – but delivery remains difficult.

OC's response: Our estates are proving that clean energy and conservation can, and should, coexist. Wind turbines alongside woodlands. Solar beside species-rich grasslands. We've ended the false choice between energy and ecology. They're co-pilots in the same mission.

6. From offsets to outcomes

Global shift: Environmental, Social, and Governance (ESG) is growing up. Investors are demanding hard evidence, not hand waving. Impact must be real, measurable, and material.

OC's response: We deliver verifiable environmental and social impact. Remote sensing, ecological monitoring, outcome-linked deals – every claim is evidenced. We don't just tell stories. We show receipts.

7. The purpose revolution

Global shift: The best talent is walking away from soulless jobs. People want meaning over money, and impact over status.

OC's response: We're not just hiring, we're building a movement. Our team is a tribe of rebels, dreamers, and doers. Ecologists, economists, entrepreneurs, and dealmakers, united by a shared purpose. We offer the chance to do the best work of your life, for the most meaningful reason imaginable.

8. The end of geography

Global shift: Remote work has decoupled talent from place. The best people don't all live in one postcode, and they don't have to.

OC's response: Our team spans mountain, coast, city, and moor. We operate as a distributed force of nature, deeply local but globally minded. We're rooted in the landscapes we love, not limited by them. That's given us a serious talent advantage.

9. The age of collaboration

Global shift: The complexity of today's challenges – climate, biodiversity, inequality – requires radical collaboration. The age of lone disruptors is over.

OC's response: We don't go it alone. Our model is built on collaboration: across sectors, landscapes, and communities. From landowners and scientists to investors and non-governmental organisations (NGOs), we treat partnerships as catalysts, not compromises, because the future is co-created, or not created at all.

10. Data is now destiny

Global shift: Conservation is no longer just a cause, it's a data-driven business. Outcomes need proof. Scale demands systems.

OC's response: Every decision we make, from acquisition to restoration, is powered by evidence. Satellite imagery, light detection and ranging (LiDAR), machine learning, and boots-on-the-ground monitoring drive our impact. Data doesn't just back us up, it leads the way.

Building at the edge of the curve

Here's the twist we didn't expect: the story of Oxygen Conservation was never just about land, markets, carbon, or trees; it was about timing. We thought we were building a conservation company. Turns out, we were building a platform for change.

The signs were always there – broken systems, shifting markets, a generation running towards meaning, not away from it – but it wasn't until *Pattern Breakers* gave us the language that we realised what we were really doing: living in the future and building what's missing. What started as a response to change has become a catalyst for it. We don't just navigate inflection points, we've begun to create them. That reframes everything that came before.

The real punchline is this: we didn't break the pattern by accident. We broke it because it was already broken, and we had the courage, the capital, the team, and the insight to build something better.

We're not just navigating the shift. We are the shift.

This is only the beginning.

On reflection

People often ask how Oxygen Conservation came to be, as if there was a single spark or a perfect origin story. While we, of course, have one, the truth is more interesting.

This business was only possible because of a convergence of so many inflection points that reshaped the world around us and created a window that had never existed before. Climate becoming financial risk, nature becoming valued, subsidies collapsing, rural life shifting, energy transforming, data accelerating, talent searching for purpose. We didn't just respond to these forces. We recognised them early, named them, and built into them with conviction.

Oxygen Conservation wasn't born from luck or linear planning. It emerged because the world was breaking and rebuilding at the same time, and we had the courage, the capital, and the culture to step into that gap. These inflection points didn't just shape our story. They made it possible, and they continue to define the path we are choosing to build next.

Completely Unreasonable: Building a High-Performance Culture for Conservation

Written June 2025

What if the most radical thing you could do for the planet wasn't planting trees or reintroducing beavers, but building the best damn team in the world to do it? This might sound like heresy in the nature sector, but if we want to Scale Conservation, truly scale it, not just talk about it at conferences, then our culture, our people, and the way we work are just as important as our projects – more so, in fact.

At Oxygen Conservation, we think of team building the same way a Michelin-starred chef thinks about food: as an art, a strategy, and an obsession. We don't want to be good at it. We want to be unreasonably good. That means going far beyond the conventional.

The dopamine of over delivery

There are moments I keep coming back to. The team delivered more than I thought possible, an incredible innovation that they'd had no idea how to produce. They exceeded expectations, and when they shared it with me, I got the same dopamine rush they did. We were buzzing. It wasn't just about the work. It was about the standard. The audacity. The ambition. The sense of shared achievement. Yes, we all applauded; our team meetings are noisy.

Those moments? They're addictive. They're what happens when you have overachievers working together with purpose. When people care, really care, about doing something well – and doing it together – it multiplies.

High performance isn't just a metric. It's a feeling. It's momentum. It's the incredible energy that happens when excellence becomes the norm. To get that, you need to build a culture that demands high standards. Loves them. Celebrates them and then raises them.

Recruiting for the ceiling, not the floor

At Oxygen Conservation, we don't hire to plug gaps. We hire to raise the roof.

That means we're looking for people who can grow faster than the company. People who are ambitious, adaptable, curious, and kind. People who not only want to win, but want to win together.

Every moment in our recruitment process is deliberate and purposeful. The process itself is long, detailed, and hard. Not because we enjoy bureaucracy (we hate it), but because we care deeply about the people we bring in and the team they will be joining. We know the biggest impact we can have on culture is who we choose to invite into it, and we make that decision every day.

We're not just hiring for today. We're building for a decade. The best hires change the trajectory of the whole business. That's why we refuse to lower the bar, even when it's tempting. *Especially* when it's tempting. Think about that hard-to-fill role, that difficult geography, that time that it's just easier to settle, *do not do it*!

One of our favourite stories concerns a candidate who was late for her interview due to a road closure, even though she had tested the route the day before to make sure she'd be on time. That combination of care, humility, and preparation, and the fact that she was open enough to share the entire story, that's culture. She's now running one of our most iconic award-winning estates.

Speak it into existence

Culture is built in language. It lives in how we talk about performance, about feedback, about learning. It's in the metaphors we use, the phrases we repeat, the mantras we adopt.

For example:

- 'Working with purpose, on purpose.'
- 'How you do anything is how you do everything.'
- 'Recruiting for the ceiling.'
- 'Be kind, especially when it's hard.'

These aren't slogans. They're reminders. A cultural GPS.

I believe you can speak things into existence. We do. Every day. From the way we describe feedback to the way we welcome new hires, we're constantly reinforcing what it means to be part of our team.

We talk about performance constantly. We don't hide from it. We embrace it. Because performance isn't just how you deliver impact. It's how you earn trust. It's how you Scale Conservation.

Purpose, on purpose

People want to work on something that matters. Not vaguely, but deeply.

Conservation matters, nature matters, but let's be clear: purpose alone is not enough. People need to work with purpose on purpose. That means knowing the mission, aligning with it, and then being trusted to deliver on it. Autonomy with accountability. Clarity with care.

The best people don't need micromanagement, and they certainly don't want it. They need trust, tools, and the room to move fast. At every performance review, I ask the senior team where I am getting in their way, and where they need more support.

We've designed our onboarding process as a welcome to a performance environment, not a paperwork exercise. It begins with a recruit's first contact with the Oxygen Conservation brand, whether this is an image, an article, a podcast, or a book. From the first conversation, new hires are invited into a story bigger than themselves. They're made to feel special, because they are, literally, the 0.1%.

Then we get to work.

Performance is a three-tier game

At Oxygen Conservation, we divide performance into three tiers:

1. **Elite performance:** A team member raises the standard for everyone. They lead by example. They perform for the team, not just in it.

2. **High performance:** A team member consistently delivers excellence in their role. They're a cultural asset.
3. **Performing elsewhere:** A team member is good. Maybe even great, but not here, not now.

This isn't about hierarchy. It's about honesty. Transparency. Clarity. People want to know how they're doing. They want to grow. They want feedback that helps them win.

When someone needs to be performing elsewhere, we don't punish them. More often than not, everybody knows this, especially the person in question. We help them find their next adventure with dignity, respect, and speed. How we exit people matters just as much as how we hire them.

This might surprise you, but we are obsessed with kindness. Not the fluffy kind. The fierce kind. Kindness that tells the truth. Kindness that expects a lot, and helps people get there.

The people strategy at Oxygen Conservation is designed to hold high standards and provide deep support. We want our team to feel challenged, stretched, and appreciated. That's why we invest so heavily in learning and development, coaching, culture-building, recognition, and reward. We don't do this because it looks good. We do it because it works. Because culture is the most scalable form of performance management.

Make it addictive

At Oxygen Conservation, we talk a lot about addictive experiences. In hospitality, in storytelling, in work. The kind of experiences people want more of. Where they feel proud, stretched, connected.

A high-performance culture should feel like that. Not always easy, but always meaningful. Always energising.

We want people to look forward to Mondays. To feel like they're part of a team that's going somewhere and doing something. To feel, as one team member said, 'like I'm part of something that actually matters' and 'I can't believe I get to do this, with these people'.

That's the goal. We're not here to create jobs. We're here to create impact.

This is the work. This is the culture. This is how we Scale Conservation. Unreasonably.

This article was inspired by the wonderful book *Unreasonable Hospitality* by Will Guidara (2022), gifted to me by Peter Harker, a partner at Saffrey, and one of the leading minds and kindest people working in the Natural Capital Sector.

On reflection

As a leader, when you offer a call to action to a business or a team, you hope it resonates, inspires, or connects. The word unreasonable has done way more than that at Oxygen Conservation; it has defined our entire approach to hospitality.

No one has taken the philosophy of unreasonable hospitality and brought it to life more than one of Oxygen Conservation's estate managers, Archie Barnes. Archie has transformed woodland clearings into pop-up cafes, tumble-down barns into high-end restaurants, wildlife safaris into exotic adventures, and seemingly everyday moments into extra special experiences by finding the unique detail no one else sees and elevating it into something people never forget.

What strikes me most is how the idea of being unreasonable stopped being a call to action for Oxygen Conservation and became a cultural operating system. I hoped the word would inspire people. Instead, it defines us. It has shaped how we recruit, how we deliver, how we show up for each other, and how we create experiences that feel unforgettable.

TWO

The Trillion-Pound Opportunity: Re-Pricing The Planet

Paying to Pollute? Only If You're in the Wrong Market

Written June 2025

For a long time, I didn't understand why some people held such negative opinions about carbon credits. I heard it all the time: 'They're just paying to continue polluting', and I thought people were missing the point. However, recently I realised they're not actually wrong. They're just talking about the wrong kind of carbon credits.

What they're usually referring to are compliance carbon credits, the realm of heavy industry and power generation, where companies are legally required to buy credits. In that sense, yes, they really are just paying to continue polluting.

That's the problem. While they may share a name, compliance and voluntary carbon credits are not the same thing. Same label. Different products. One is about permission. The other is about progress. Lumping them together creates confusion, fuels criticism, and risks throwing out something incredibly valuable in the process.

Let's break it down.

Compliance carbon markets

The compliance market is the world of cap-and-trade, where companies buy permission slips to keep emitting greenhouse gases. Think of it like paying your water bill: obligatory, transactional, and devoid of anything else.

These credits don't represent carbon being removed from the atmosphere. They're about staying within legal limits and paying more if you pollute more. It's compliance economics, a system designed to incentivise doing less harm while making it more expensive to do more harm, not create more good.

No tangible restoration. No net gain. Just accounting. Just permission.

Voluntary carbon markets

With the voluntary market, businesses and individuals *choose* to invest in the removal or avoidance of carbon emissions. You can think of it like ordering sparkling water in a beautifully blown glass bottle at a restaurant, supporting jobs in that restaurant and the glass-blowing industry. You don't *have* to. You *choose* to, and you pay more for it. Crucially, you can't just turn on the tap and expect sparkling water to come out.

These two systems aren't interchangeable. Compliance credits are designed for a specific group of large emitters – power plants and industrial giants – operating in a closed loop. The average business, let alone individual, can't and shouldn't access them.

Voluntary credits, on the other hand, are open. Accessible. Impact-led. They exist to fund tangible, measurable environmental restoration – projects that remove carbon and deliver far more than climate benefits. In our analogy, while what comes out of the glass bottle and out of the tap is technically water, there is no price correlation between the two. Your utility bill going up doesn't suddenly make your bottle of San Pellegrino more expensive. Same category, but a completely different product. No price linkage. No substitution.

Voluntary credits fund real boots-in-the-mud projects. Planting woodlands. Restoring peatlands. Rewetting wetlands. Regenerating soils. They don't just sequester carbon, they slow floodwaters. Cool rivers. Shelter wildlife. Create green jobs rebuilding rural economies left behind by the race to the bottom.

When done right, *and it must be done right,* voluntary carbon credits aren't an excuse or a get-out clause. They're a contribution.

Premium impact, premium price

Voluntary credits are smaller in scale than compliance credits but can be much higher in value. That's the point. They're not a mass-market compliance product. They're a high-integrity choice for businesses that want to lead, not lag.

There's an important word in that statement: 'can'. Unlike with compliance credits, where every allowance to pollute is the same as another, in the voluntary market, every credit is different. Some of them are produced by schemes with dubious methodologies that support questionable practices, and some are delivering real-world carbon impact as well as huge environmental and social impact.

Low-quality voluntary credits cost less than compliance credits. In fact, they shouldn't be allowed at all, and we are seeing increasingly that these types of credits are being rejected by the market. However, the high-quality credits, the ones that restore nature and provide a positive environmental and social impact, in addition to carbon removal, are priced higher than compliance credits as organisations are increasingly willing to invest in schemes that deliver real value.

High-quality voluntary credits reflect environmental ambition, but also brand values, corporate culture, and a willingness to be part of the solution. When used well, they're bought *in addition* to reducing internal emissions, not as a replacement. The best companies don't buy credits to avoid responsibility. They do it to scale their impact.

This isn't a shortcut. It's a statement.

The real problem isn't carbon – it's communication

Let's acknowledge something important: this stuff is complicated and confusing. The fact that both compliance and voluntary credits are called carbon credits is part of the problem. It fuels cynicism and makes it all too easy to misjudge something that, when done properly, has the power to deliver real, lasting change.

Like so many things in the environment sector, carbon credits don't merely have a trust problem. They have a communication problem.

This isn't just about policy, pricing, or permanence. It's about storytelling. It's about helping people understand *what they're buying, why it matters,* and *what it enables*. The voluntary market doesn't just need high integrity, it needs better marketing.

That's something all of us – project developers, businesses, buyers, advocates, critics – need to help fix. If we let confusion win, we'll lose one of the few tools we have that can fund nature-based solutions at scale, right now.

No, it's not perfect, but if you're looking for a reason not to act, you'll find one. If you're looking for a reason to make progress, high-quality voluntary carbon credits offer a solution.

On reflection

If tap water vs sparkling water doesn't work for you, please feel free to substitute in an alternative analogy, perhaps your television licence and Sky TV, or your standing charge for energy and power from renewable energy suppliers. I'd love to hear your analogies.

Stop Trying to Shame People into Caring About the Environment

Written July 2025

There's a pervasive sound echoing through the sustainability space, and it's not the wail of a world in crisis, it's the quiet yawn of disinterest. A long, tired, involuntary yawn from an audience worn down by guilt-laden messaging, hollow slogans, and statistics that blur into background noise.

Here's the uncomfortable truth: we've taken the most urgent and transformational issue of our time and reduced it to a tedious, moralistic monologue. Our messaging triggers guilt instead of curiosity. We've wrapped our stories in hazard tape when we should have been opening doors.

In our haste to avert ecological collapse, we forgot the most compelling tool we have: an engaging, inspiring, adventurous story.

The environment sector has a marketing problem

This isn't a funding problem. It's not a science problem. It's a narrative failure.

In just two days, I spoke in three vastly different rooms – business, political, creative – and heard the same recycled talking points. The same monotony. The same echo chamber of climate rhetoric that flatters insiders and alienates everyone else.

Too often, we're congratulating ourselves for simply existing in the environmental space. We're fixated on performative wokeness and virtue-signalling through trivial actions, like bragging about a £10,000 win or a ceremonial tree planting as if it's systemic change.

Meanwhile, the sector (if we can even call ourselves a sector yet – great question asked by Guy Thompson, MD of EnTrade, on his 2025 episode of the Shoot Room Sessions) is miles away from building the kind of credible, compelling products or stories that today's investors actually need. We cry out for capital while refusing to articulate returns. If we're not even trying to provide a return, it's not an investment, it's a donation. We talk about scaling while sidestepping the conversation on value, and still, astonishingly, we apologise for wanting to make a profit!

Environmental restoration company Nattergal built on the foundations established at the rewilding project Knepp by implementing a structured operational model that attracted significant investment into the environmental sector, including £40m recently secured from Aviva. It's developed infrastructure to support large-scale ecological restoration and brought a high-integrity carbon credit to market. This credit achieved a sale price of £100 per tonne, setting a new benchmark for premium natural capital products in the UK and continuing to move the market forwards. Nattergal's approach demonstrates that credible, measurable outcomes backed by professional delivery can attract serious market attention.

Let's be honest: charities exist where capitalism has failed. They fill the gaps where society refuses to assign financial value. If we truly want to mainstream conservation, we need to stop operating like failure is noble. When are the professionals coming?

For years, we've relied on desperation as a brand strategy. We've made gloom our aesthetic and criticism our primary communication tactic. Predictably, it hasn't worked.

We cannot frighten someone into loving nature. We can't shame a person into reimagining land use. We absolutely cannot build a billion-pound natural capital market on hopelessness, fear, and despair.

We should have been crafting stories that enchant, invite, and energise. Instead, we're stunned when donations wane, political will fades, and the public tunes out, and the investment still doesn't come.

Environment-friendly company RESTORE has pioneered a different route into the natural capital market by working with existing landowners, focusing on unlocking ecological and financial value that others have failed to recognise or realise. The team has built a collaborative model that empowers landholders to rethink what's possible, and to take part in environmental recovery on the land that they know and love.

Fear isn't fuel – it's a fire extinguisher

Think about it: clothing brands don't sell sustainable jackets by showing homeless people freezing on the streets, drinks companies don't advertise with images of people dying of thirst, so why does the environmental sector keep trying to inspire action through despair?

Brands like Patagonia and Finisterre succeed not by showcasing catastrophe, but by selling aspiration. They invite people into a lifestyle; a world where adventure and beauty intersect with responsibility. Their imagery uplifts, it doesn't scold.

Even Patagonia, with all its activist credibility earned from financial strength, rarely leads with fear. Its team has earned (literally) the right to be bold, and yet their stories still centre on awe and action, not apocalypse. At Oxygen Conservation, we've chosen a similar path, and that's how we were able to sell a product that has achieved a new high point for premium carbon credits.

Here's the truth: no investor funds desperation. They fund potential. They invest in compelling visions. They want to be part of something dynamic, scalable, and meaningfully impactful.

Environment Bank is professionalising the BNG market by bringing institutional credibility, investment rigour, and operational scale to a sector that's often been fragmented and underpowered. By working in partnership with farmers (as opposed to attacking and criticising them) and developing habitat banks to fulfil BNG requirements, the team has created compelling alternative investment opportunities. In a space once filled with uncertainty, they've brought stability and confidence, backed by the institutional weight of asset manager Gresham House, and they have done it without shame, blame, or vilification.

That's why we at Oxygen Conservation transformed our shoot room into a podcast studio. Why we share stories of rainforest restoration, rewilded landscapes, and reenergised rural communities. Why we pour as much passion into our storytelling as we do into our environmental work. Yes, we are proud to champion this sector, and to spotlight the incredible talent it's attracting.

When we can talk about these aspects of what we do, why would we choose the same tired rhetoric? We should be better than that, and the sector is getting there.

Rewilding Wealth means rewriting the script

At Oxygen Conservation, we're not only building a conservation company; we're also building a market-shaping brand. A professional, high-performance business that fuses ecological restoration with high-quality imagery, videography, and storytelling. We want to become a powerhouse of profitability and purpose, unapologetically blending bold ideas with business rigour, because we believe that to be a good business, we have to be *in* business.

We are not here for self-congratulations or to feel better about ourselves. We are here to outperform expectations; environmentally, socially, and financially. In our world, conservation doesn't rely on charity, it competes with the best commercial investments in the world. Protection is not a cost; it's a value proposition. A revenue generator. A growth story. The biggest economic opportunity of our time.

In a sector where most ecological consultants criticise the system, CEO Cain Blythe and the CreditNature team have chosen to work with regulators, not against them. They have engaged directly with the Scottish Government over many years; listening, learning, sharing, and teaching, all to build the frameworks needed to value nature from within the system itself, and they've done it with a level of commitment, drive, and patience that's rare in this space. It's wonderful to see their increasing success in shaping the future of nature markets.

Enough with the platitudes and terrible templates. Let's dismantle the myth that doing good means doing without. Let's build brands that speak the language of investors and environmentalists alike: clear, credible, compelling. Let's tell stories that sell, not with shame, but with strategy. Not with fear, but with ambition. Not everyone will like it, but do you think they like what we're doing now either?

We've tried despair and got disinterest. It's time to stop shaming people into caring and start building a future they want to be part of...

On reflection

The following article should be read in reflection.

Collaborative Competition: Why I'm Happy to Be the Biggest Cheerleader for the Natural Capital Sector

Written August 2025

One of the questions I get asked most often is: why are you so supportive of other organisations and people in the natural capital sector? Aren't they your competition?

The answer is: of course they are, but why can't we compete collaboratively? We're all trying to solve the same problems: the climate crisis, the biodiversity collapse, the fact that nature has been undervalued and under attack for centuries. At Oxygen Conservation, we've always been committed to making the market for natural capital because we believe it has the best potential to deliver genuine positive environmental and social impact, and if that's true, then my role is to cheer louder, push harder, and celebrate every single success that moves us all closer to that future.

I believe, deeply, that to run a good business, we have to be *in* business, and that means a profitable business.

Not profit at all costs, but profit as the result of doing something valuable. That's why I've always argued for regenerative capitalism, a model where reward and recognition flow to those creating value through a triple bottom line: people, planet, and profit.

This means making sure that those who are restoring rivers, reviving rainforests, rejuvenating soils, and rebuilding biodiversity can make a wonderful living that's not just sustainable, but inspiring. The more we collectively succeed, the more we raise the bar for everyone; collaborative competition in action.

In sport, the best rivalries push players to new levels – in tennis, Federer needed Nadal; in football, Ronaldo needed Messi. Teams need worthy opponents to sharpen them. In the same way, the natural capital sector wins when we compete to lift each other higher.

A better way to live and work

For me, this is about more than economics. It's about people. One of the best callings you can possibly have is to create an environment where wonderful people can build rewarding, positively impactful, and inspiring lives. That's what drives me and what drives Oxygen Conservation. It's also why I want to champion everyone else in this space.

Every time someone succeeds in creating a new wetland, financing a peatland project, or proving that natural capital investment works, it creates more space for more people to live lives of impact and purpose. In a competitive marketplace, the wins of others don't diminish ours; they make the whole sector bigger, stronger, and more diverse, ultimately helping us solve our shared problems: the climate crisis and the biodiversity collapse.

Criticism comes with the territory

Many people in this sector have been criticised, attacked, even vilified for trying to do things differently. For speaking the truth to institutional power and challenging regulatory roadblocks. For refusing to play by the same rules that have broken our climate and driven us towards mass extinction. Examples might include buying land at scale, daring to integrate renewable energy alongside wood creation projects, or suggesting the sector should be a profitable, high-performance environment.

I've lived that reality too and I've come to realise that criticism is not just unavoidable, it's a sign we're on the right path. If we're not rattling cages, we're probably not doing enough. The key is how we respond: with persistence, positivity, and the courage to keep going. Because when we turn criticism into fuel, it powers us forward, and that momentum lifts the entire sector.

Competition through collaboration

I once wrote about collaboration not competition, and I've regretted that line ever since. What I should have written was collaborative competition.

The natural capital economy is still in its infancy. It's new, messy, and being watched by a world desperate for solutions. That means every win matters. Every credible project, every successful investment, every new standard or framework that proves this can work matters.

Oxygen Conservation's purpose isn't just to Scale Conservation. It's to make the market.

I do appreciate this is a unique perspective for this market at this time. In the same way that Elon Musk openly shared ideas and even blueprints for electric vehicles (EVs), realising the real challenge wasn't building the best EV but building the entire market; we too recognise that necessity. If natural capital already existed in a conventional mature market, I'd tend to agree with the sentiments of entrepreneur and investor Peter Thiel that competition leads only to globalisation, commodification, and lower prices that depress a sector (2015), but we're nowhere near that point. Instead, I can proudly cheerlead for the entire sector, and that is one of my favourite things about getting to do this right now.

You can't make a market alone. You need a sector. You need a movement. You need a cheering crowd. Yes, you need competition, but the kind that sharpens ideas, raises standards, and fuels momentum rather than stifling it.

That's why I'm more than happy to play the role of biggest cheerleader. This isn't about me, or even about Oxygen Conservation. It's about building something so much bigger – a new economy where protecting and restoring nature is not only possible, but inevitable. A place where we compete to do more good at speed and where collaboration is our competitive edge.

I'll keep cheering, and competing, until we get there.

On reflection

It would be pretty ridiculous to write this article without cheerleading for some of the wonderful businesses in the sector right now, so here goes…

Triodos for being the first UK bank to fund natural capital at scale; Nattergal for bringing serious institutional investment to the sector; RESTORE, offering a purely ecological approach to natural capital; Rebalance Earth, connecting natural infrastructure and resilience with finance in groundbreaking ways; Great Yellow, pioneering new ways of thinking about natural capital; Credit Nature, building trusted high-integrity credits that give nature measurable value; and Tree Story, reminding us all that planting and growing trees can be deeply personal as well as globally important. These are the kinds of organisations that make me proud to be their cheerleader, because every step they take forward moves the whole sector further, faster.

Are We Sure We're Not Greenwashing the Truth?

Written July 2025

As the world of conservation continues to reform towards a professional natural capital economy, many long-standing beliefs are still accepted without scrutiny. These ideas, often presented as best practices or common sense, can become ingrained not because they are effective, but because they feel safe and familiar. However, when we examine them through the lens of real-world application – across ecosystems, investment environments, government policy, and the realities of working with local communities – we tend to find that these ideas fall short of delivering meaningful impact (and of reality itself).

Much of what is deemed standard practice is actually just tradition repackaged. The term 'consensus' often masks an unwillingness to make hard decisions, while 'strategy' is regularly wheeled out to justify a growing collection of workshops, stakeholder engagement sessions, and badly drawn diagrams. Now is not the time to fall into the trap of performative progress, like the all-too-familiar planning meeting that results only in scheduling yet another planning meeting. Prioritise action over process, and make sure that every discussion drives a tangible outcome rather than just extending the timeline.

This piece is a call to challenge the ideas we accept too easily. To recognise the complexities and contradictions. Because real progress requires us to move beyond our intellectual comfort zones and actually build an entire new economic ecosystem.

Seventeen uncomfortable truths

1. **We don't treat nature as priceless, we treat it as worthless.** Despite rhetoric around nature's 'priceless' value, we largely exclude it from our financial frameworks, which leads to its continued exploitation. The absence of natural capital accounting perpetuates the illusion that ecological assets can be depleted without consequence.
2. **The environment sector doesn't really want investment.** Although many call for private sector investment, they often reject the very structures that attract it. Philanthropy dominates, while entrepreneurial approaches are viewed with scepticism or openly criticised. The perception that financial returns are inherently misaligned with ecological goals continues to limit access to broader capital markets and private sector innovation.
3. **Profit is not a dirty word.** To attract the innovation and talent required for transformative change, conservation must be seen as a viable and valuable investment opportunity. When profitability and

ecological restoration align, momentum accelerates and talent follows.

4. **Small projects might be big distractions.** While these initiatives may feel meaningful and are relatively easy to deliver, they can quietly drain time, resources, and momentum from the larger systemic interventions that actually shift baselines. A press release celebrating a small isolated win doesn't excite serious investment, it simply highlights the absence of scale, ambition, and a coordinated strategy.

   For those delivering conservation on the ground, this is a reminder that ambition shouldn't be scary or unattainable. It's a challenge to step up and think bigger.

5. **Sustainability was a missed opportunity.** Maintaining the current state of ecosystems is no longer enough. We need to actively restore and enhance natural systems and processes that have already been degraded. Regeneration is not just ecological; it's economic, environmental, social, and cultural.

6. **We've all actively funded environmental destruction.** For decades, public money has propped up agricultural and land management practices that have systematically degraded ecosystems. Historic agri-environment schemes have been painfully generic and deliberately 'easy', designed to reward ownership over restoration, and to maintain the status quo rather than challenge it.

   Reform isn't just overdue – it's urgent. Aligning subsidies with environmental outcomes isn't radical;

it's common sense. It's ethical, economically sound, and strategically necessary if we're serious about reversing the damage we've all paid for.

7. **Farmers are not custodians of the landscape.** The idea that farmers are natural custodians of the landscape is a romantic narrative, one rooted more in nostalgia than evidence. While some individuals strive for sustainability, the truth is that farming, particularly at scale, has done more damage to the natural environment than almost any other land use.

   This isn't solely the fault of farmers. We've all played a part by funding the very system, through decades of subsidies, that encouraged overproduction, overextraction, and ecological degradation. It's time we acknowledged both the economic realities farmers operate within and the environmental consequences of the incentives we've designed.

8. **Access to private land requires accountability.** Many landowners are hesitant to open up their properties because of public misuse. Broader access must be paired with public education, mutual responsibility, and economic protection. Without shared values and respect for landscapes, access can lead to degradation rather than connection. If the public wants access to their land, private landowners should be protected by public funding.

9. **We don't celebrate progress, we punish the absence of perfection.** We've created a culture that punishes people for not being perfect. Instead of celebrating those who try to reduce their environmental impact, we criticise their imperfections. This attitude discourages innovation and silences good intentions.

Progress comes from action, not flawless execution, and it's time to reward the effort to do better, not just the appearance of being right.

10. **We too often prioritise activity over actual impact.** The sector regularly calls for another strategy or another report not because it lacks answers, but because the answers lead to difficult conversations that might upset people. Avoiding discomfort has become an excuse for inaction. Instead, we prioritise activity over actual impact.
11. **Funding bureaucracies only leads to more bureaucracy.** Providing additional funding to Natural England or any other regulator, often rightly criticised for bureaucracy, won't solve the problem. More money doesn't mean better outcomes; it usually means more paperwork, more delay, and more institutional drag. Reform, not expansion, is what's urgently needed.
12. **Scotland's deep political and cultural obsession with land reform could cost the Earth.** It could even undermine the very environmental and economic outcomes it seeks to champion.

    Without clear alignment with market-based mechanisms for natural capital, such reform risks destabilising property markets, deterring long-term investment, and stalling the development of a robust nature-based economy. The impact of this on people, wildlife, and the natural world will be catastrophic. Policymakers must resist the temptation of short-term optics and build reforms on practical, investable foundations, or risk missing a generational opportunity, again.

13. **Volunteerism is trapping the nature sector in the amateur world.** Volunteerism and passion may be rooted in good intentions, but when they are a substitute for structure and accountability, they reinforce the perception of conservation as an amateur pursuit. This undermines the sector's credibility, diminishes trust from investors and policymakers, and stalls the growth of professional expertise essential to solving complex environmental challenges.
14. **The number of environmental NGOs is evidence of failure.** We only need environmental charities because the environment is undervalued. Their very existence reflects our failure to embed nature within functional market mechanisms. When protection depends on philanthropy, it's because systems have failed to price nature properly. More NGOs doesn't tend to mean more impact, but more fragmentation and duplication, and a continued dependence on the idea that saving nature is something extra, not essential.
15. **The idea of the local community doesn't work in a diverse modern world.** *'But what do local people think?'* is a question I hear regularly, yet few confront the complexity behind it. The idea of a unified 'community' is more comforting than accurate. Most places are made up of a mosaic of interests, experiences, and needs. Some people are empowered and vocal, while others are underrepresented or silenced. Assuming consensus or cohesion can lead to misinformed decisions and superficial engagement. True listening requires acknowledging conflict, power dynamics, and historical context, not just giving airtime to the loudest or most familiar voices.

16. **Public consultations are being weaponised.** Consultations are meant to democratise decision making, but all too often, they distort it. Well-intentioned feedback processes are frequently captured by the most vocal, organised, or aggrieved participants, not the most informed or representative. This creates an echo chamber of influence, where policy and funding decisions skew towards narrow self-interest rather than public good.
17. **The idea of consensus is simply not possible in today's complex world.** The pursuit of consensus rewards inaction, waters down vision, and creates a false sense of unity. Strong, informed leadership sometimes requires moving ahead despite disagreement, because progress and positive impact don't come with unanimous applause.

At Oxygen Conservation, we are committed not only to positive environmental and social impact, but also to evolving the mindsets and structures that govern conservation itself. We operate in a space of constant iteration, learning from our experiences and challenging outdated norms. True progress does not depend on universal agreement. It begins with honesty and intellectual courage. The kind that acknowledges complexity and embraces discomfort as part of the path to better outcomes.

If some of these statements feel confronting, it is because within this discomfort lies the opportunity for the environmental sector to grow more resilient, more ambitious, and more aligned with the realities of our time. Let us keep interrogating assumptions, evolving our models, and remaining open to uncomfortable but necessary truths. Only then can we build a future that truly works, for people, for nature, and for the planet.

On reflection

I'd like to offer an eighteenth uncomfortable truth that has emerged throughout the fierce debate surrounding land ownership in Scotland.

18. **A small but vocal minority dislike the idea that effort and value creation should be rewarded**. They resent capitalism, disdain the idea that effort and achievement should matter, and object to the notion that those who create value ought to benefit most from it.

That ideology matters because it shapes policy. In early November 2025, the Scottish Government passed the Land Reform (Scotland) Bill (now the Land Reform [Scotland] Act 2025) with the stated aim of widening land ownership. Yet, as leading lawyer Don Macleod has observed, the legislation falls short of that promise, and during the legislative process he went as far as describing it as 'junk law', characterising the proposals as a series of unworkable compromises that would satisfy almost nobody (Connell, 2025).

The Land Reform Bill's aim of increasing the number of people owning land in Scotland implies that how many people own something matters more than what they do with it, however good. Through the debate around this bill, the topic of natural capital was attacked by a small number of elected officials who seek to resist positive progress and change and instead criticise natural capital as being an extractive concept. In the next piece, I discredit that unsubstantiated claim.

The Great Extraction Delusion

Written November 2025

There is a strange and persistent accusation thrown at natural capital: that it is extractive. That investing in landscapes, restoring ecosystems, and revitalising rural economies is somehow the same as mining, mono-cropping, and deep-sea dredging. It is an argument so wildly incoherent that it survives only because repeating something loudly has always been easier than understanding it deeply, and yet, here we are. Let's deal with this directly, with the level of precision and unapologetic honesty the conversation deserves.

Calling natural capital extractive is not just wrong. It is a moral campaign against capitalism itself, dressed up as an environmental issue. It is an ideological hangover from a worldview that cannot imagine a system where doing good and doing well are anything other than mutually exclusive.

This worldview might have belonged in the twentieth century. It certainly has no place in a world that needs more investment in nature, not less.

The value we create

Here is the reality of what we at Oxygen Conservation actually do. We buy land that has often been degraded for generations. Within the next few years, we will have planted millions of trees in landscapes where native woodland has been erased. We restore peatlands that were drained, burned, or ignored. We create new habitats where biodiversity has collapsed. We hire people. We pay them well. We provide homes and improve properties to support rural living. We proactively invest in economies by hiring local contractors, supporting rural supply chains, and inviting visitors to reconnect with landscapes that have long been locked away.

What exactly has been extracted? Diversity? No. We add it. Soil health? No. We improve it. Communities? No. We create employment. Opportunity? No. We increase it. Value? Yes, but only after creating it first.

The work speaks for itself. Sixty new jobs across our portfolio. Dozens of rural businesses scaling because of our investment. Partnerships with TreeStory, Caledonian Climate Partners, Taiga Upland, and many others. The restoration of habitats that had been written off as ecological losses. The creation of ecotourism opportunities for people who want to experience wildness rather than merely read about it.

Extraction is about taking without giving. What we do is the opposite. We give first. Capital flows into landscapes, not out of them. We build, repair, restore and renew. It takes risk and requires patience, because nature does not move at the pace of financial quarters.

Yes, we receive government support. The government has also supported farmers for decades, and continues to support the fossil fuels industry, notwithstanding the UK Parliament declaring a climate emergency in 2019.

The support we receive is essential while the natural capital economy is developing – one day it will not be required at all – and is used to deliver positive environmental outcomes. We restore peat, rewet wetlands, establish native woodlands, and regenerate habitats that have been declining for years. If that is objectionable, then the complaint is not about us. It is about reality.

Leave the old narratives in the past

The most ironic part is this. Natural capital is accused of being extractive by many of the same voices that quietly tolerated – even supported – the actual extraction of the past century. Soil stripped of organic life. Watercourses straightened and degraded. Native species eradicated. Moorlands burned. Rivers polluted. Communities hollowed out by economic decline. Somehow all of that was fine. A blind eye was turned, but restoring what was destroyed? That is the real threat.

The logic collapses under its own weight.

We create ecological value, social value, and economic value. Investors share in that value only after it has been created and only after communities, ecosystems, and local economies have benefited first. That is not extraction. It is investment in its truest form.

Of course, investment carries risk. It is slow. It is demanding. It is capital deployed with long-term conviction. Should those who take this risk be rewarded? Absolutely. Incentives matter. Performance matters. Accountability matters. The emerging natural capital economy is proving a truth that many do not want to acknowledge. Profit and positive impact do not compete. They compound. They rise together.

To call that extractive is lazy. It is a refusal to accept that capitalism can evolve into something regenerative. It is a fear that if this model succeeds, old narratives fail, and they should fail. They have failed landscapes, failed rural communities, and failed the planet.

We are not extracting anything. We are repairing what others extracted. We are restoring landscapes to life. We are proving that conservation can be a high-performance, investable asset class. We are demonstrating that the fastest way to restore ecosystems at scale is to align nature's outcomes with economic outcomes.

The extractive accusation is not just wrong. It is irrelevant. The work is bigger than the criticism. If critics want to see extraction, they can study the past. If they want to see regeneration, they can look at what we are doing right now.

This is not exploitation. This is investment with intent. This is capital with a conscience. This is how you Scale Conservation.

On reflection

In 2025, Scotland passed landmark legislation to introduce new standards of transparency, community benefit, and environmental accountability for large landholders. The land management requirements that will be introduced by the Land Reform (Scotland) Bill align with what we've been building at Oxygen Conservation since day one. Responsible, transparent nature-positive ownership isn't just advantageous anymore. It's the benchmark.

For years, we've argued that conservation must be scalable, measurable, and investable. That the only way to make protecting the planet more profitable than destroying it is to link management to outcomes. Now, Scotland has written that principle into law.

As our chairman, Benny Higgins, wrote previously in *The Times* (2025):

> *'It has become all too easy to cast large estates in a light that is far from modern reality: that rural estates are relics from a bygone age. As chairman of Buccleuch [and Oxygen Conservation], I oversee a business, not in substance unlike other businesses I have managed, that sets out to support jobs that are essential to families, focuses on our communities and understands the needs of our environment. We must not allow dated characterisations of the world of estate management to misinform decision-making. The world has moved on.'*

Adapting to lead

Let's be clear: this act, once implemented, will change how large rural estates are structured, managed, and sold. For some, that will be uncomfortable. It challenges inherited models and invites scrutiny that not everyone will welcome. It will potentially slow the market, make land transactions more costly and complex, and create a barrier to future private investment into rural Scotland.

We may not agree with some of the principles behind the act, nor the way it has been drafted. However, it represents an important step forward for those of us who believe in transparency, accountability, and long-term impact. Rather than a compliance burden or a transactional constraint, perhaps the act is an opportunity to recognise that large-scale landholdings are, in truth, part of our national infrastructure: critical assets that underpin climate stability, energy security, flood resilience, and community wellbeing. In that sense, Oxygen Conservation's managed land isn't so different from the energy grid or transport networks. They're all essential systems that demand stewardship, performance standards, and public-interest accountability.

We regulate energy and water because society can't function without them, yet we've left land, the foundation of every other system, largely unregulated. This act could help resolve that paradox. That's a philosophy we at Oxygen Conservation can engage with as proud infrastructure operators managing essential natural systems on behalf of the nation – transparently, responsibly, and with measurable public benefit.

Regulating opportunity

Where others see complication, we see opportunity. As we understand it, the act requires 'large' landowners (1,000 hectares/2,471 acres or more in a single holding or two or more single holdings within 250m of each other) to publish land management plans with clear environmental outcomes (including how the owner intends to manage the land to adapt to climate change and increase biodiversity) and the steps taken by the owner to engage with communities in relation to the development of the plan. For us, that's an open invitation to continue showcasing what modern conservation investment looks like – to prove that responsible ownership can deliver measurable natural capital outcomes: carbon storage, biodiversity uplift, clean water, green jobs, and homes for people in rural communities.

There's also a deeper structural truth. The new land management reforms effectively reward those who already operate with scale, data, and transparency. Regulation now demands evidence and alignment – and few can prove it. For some, this is a key reason why the act was necessary. For us at Oxygen Conservation, its consequence is to reward us for recognising the natural capital opportunity in Scotland early and investing to make it a reality. While we would want to see many more high-integrity nature-based carbon projects brought forward in Scotland – they are badly needed – the impact of the act is that our premium credits will be even more distinctive.

From perceived privilege to purpose

For too long, land reform debates have been framed as a battle between privilege and power, between 'owners' and 'communities'. That debate is fundamentally flawed, and everyone loses if it continues. What Scotland is now offering is a new social contract of ownership – one where land serves people, nature, and the economy collectively, not one at the expense of the others.

In many ways, this legislation was foreshadowed by Benny when he wrote:

> *'One can only hope that ministers pursue land reform legislation that serves communities rather than gratuitously punishing landowners. We must acknowledge that landowners have embraced change over the last few decades and are heavily involved in stimulating growth in rural areas.'*

That's the philosophy Oxygen Conservation was founded on. Every acre we own is a platform for environmental improvement, community connection, and long-term value creation. Ownership, in our model, is stewardship with structure. Capital with conscience.

We often talk about rewilding wealth, taking capital that was once extractive and turning it into something regenerative. We hope this act will enable that on a national scale.

The future of land ownership

The passing of the Land Reform (Scotland) Act is historic. It will undoubtedly lead to inertia, confusion, and bureaucratic challenges. However, in the years to come, the investors who succeed will be those who embraced reform early. The landowners who thrive will be those who invite communities in, not keep them out. The organisations that lead will be those that combine purpose with performance – proving that doing good and doing well are not competing ideas, but complementary ones.

That's the future Oxygen Conservation was built for.

To ensure the act delivers the best possible outcomes for Scotland's economy and environment, we believe these twelve actions are essential for its implementation:

Policy clarity

- Act quickly and simply – implement with urgency and clarity to prevent market stagnation.
- Guarantee long-term policy stability so investors and landowners can plan with confidence.
- Meaningfully consult with landowners in the same spirit and manner that the act expects of landowners when they're engaging with local communities.
- Protect nature restoration and ensure the act does not slow or hamper the urgency of our response to the climate and biodiversity crises.

Investment confidence

- Underwrite the value of premium carbon credits to stabilise pricing and incentivise integrity.
- Mandate the polluter pays principle through nature credit purchases for the most environmentally harmful industries and all government infrastructure projects.

- Invest boldly in regenerative projects that accelerate the transition to a nature-positive economy.
- Continue large-scale grant programmes for woodland creation and peatland restoration.

Community empowerment

- Fund community land acquisition to make local people active partners in regeneration.
- Relax planning rules for sustainable homes on newly lotted land to revitalise rural economies.
- Support innovation in ecotourism, regenerative agriculture, and renewable energy.
- Position Scotland as the global leader in nature investment – where finance, conservation, and community benefit meet.

The Protector Profits Principle

Written July 2025

In recent years, a powerful shift has begun to take place: a recognition that our natural world is not just something to be preserved out of obligation, but something that has intrinsic economic value, capable of delivering significant returns for those who invest in ensuring its future. This idea, when fully realised, offers a transformative opportunity to harness the forces of the market to restore and protect our environment.

Enter the Protector Profits Principle, a concept that could reshape how we think about conservation by leveraging economic incentives to reward those who actively protect and enhance the natural world. By aligning market mechanisms with environmental outcomes, we have the potential to create a new era in which conservation becomes a viable and attractive business strategy, not a mere philanthropic endeavour. From carbon and biodiversity credits to payments for ecosystem services, the Protector Profits Principle encourages businesses, landowners, and investors to profit from being responsible stewards of our natural assets.

Conservation as an economic opportunity

Traditionally, conservation has been framed as a cost, something that comes with financial burdens and compromises, a moral pursuit that requires sacrifice. What if we could rewrite that narrative? What if conservation became synonymous with opportunity?

The Protector Profits Principle is about flipping the script and positioning nature as an integral asset within our economy. It's about recognising the vital ecosystem services – clean air, clean water, pollination, carbon sequestration – that the natural world provides and then building a financial framework that rewards individuals and companies for maintaining and enhancing those services.

The fundamental question is this: how can we make conservation pay? How do we create a system where it is in the best economic interests of landowners, businesses, and investors to protect and restore nature? The answer lies in embracing market mechanisms and putting a price on the priceless, the invaluable services that nature offers.

Natural capital markets: A growing frontier

At the heart of the Protector Profits Principle is the idea of genuinely recognising natural capital. Natural capital refers to the world's stock of natural resources – its woodlands, rivers, wetlands, and oceans – which provide the services essential for people and wildlife, and economic prosperity. The challenge is to translate the value of these services into financial terms, and in doing so, make the case for conservation as an investable asset class.

Natural capital markets, such as those for carbon and biodiversity units, represent a rapidly growing frontier in which the value of natural systems is monetised and traded. Take carbon credits, for example. When a woodland sequesters carbon, it provides a quantifiable service that has economic value in a carbon-constrained world. Carbon credits allow landowners to sell the value of that service to companies seeking to compensate for their emissions. Similarly, biodiversity units can allow landowners to generate income by enhancing habitats and supporting species recovery.

These markets make it possible to financially reward landowners for the role they play in conserving and restoring nature, effectively turning environmental stewardship into an economically viable enterprise. By connecting the private sector, investors, and conservationists, natural capital markets represent a powerful tool for scaling up nature-positive projects and bringing conservation into the economic mainstream.

From polluter pays to Protector Profits

The Protector Profits Principle builds upon the established idea of the polluter pays. Under the polluter pays framework, those who degrade the environment should be held responsible for funding its restoration, a concept that rightly emphasises accountability. However, we also need to reward those who proactively protect and enhance our natural world and improve the environment. The Protector Profits Principle ensures that those people are not only recognised, but financially rewarded for their contributions.

This principle goes beyond punitive measures and embraces the power of positive incentives. Just as taxes can be used to dissuade harmful behaviour, financial rewards can be used to encourage beneficial actions. The goal is to create an environment where landowners and businesses see tangible financial benefits from enhancing biodiversity, restoring ecosystems, and contributing to climate resilience.

For example, a farmer who adopts regenerative practices that improve soil health and biodiversity could earn biodiversity credits, which can then be sold on the open market. Similarly, an energy company that funds habitat restoration in connection with renewable energy projects could generate income from enhanced ecosystem services. The Protector Profits Principle incentivises actors across sectors to engage in conservation, not because they have to, but because it pays to do so.

However, the Protector Profits Principle goes beyond incentivising individual actions, it has the transformative potential to reshape societal norms in ways that punitive measures cannot achieve. Rewarding environmental stewardship creates a ripple effect, fostering widespread adoption and gradually building intrinsic motivation as sustainable actions become linked to shared values and tangible economic opportunities. Unlike punitive measures, which often rely on fear to enforce compliance, this principle inspires positive engagement by aligning financial rewards with long-term ecological benefits. In doing so, it drives systemic change, embedding regenerative practices at the heart of economic decision making.

Levelling up through nature-based solutions

The Protector Profits Principle also represents a powerful tool for 'levelling up' rural communities. These areas often face economic challenges due to declining industries, limited job opportunities, and clinging to a repressive status quo. By adopting a model that rewards conservation, we can create new revenue streams that support rural livelihoods while delivering environmental benefits for the whole country.

Imagine a landscape where farmers and landowners are not just producers of food or fibre, but also producers of carbon sequestration, pollinator services, and biodiversity. Payments for these services could provide much-needed income stability, making rural economies more resilient and helping to address economic disparities between urban and rural areas.

Instead of relying solely on government subsidies, rural communities could benefit from private sector investment and market-driven opportunities. The Protector Profits Principle puts money into the hands of those on the frontlines of conservation, turning our natural landscapes into hubs of economic innovation and ecological recovery.

Making the market for natural capital

The Protector Profits Principle isn't just about creating value for landowners, it's about making the market for natural capital as a legitimate investable asset class. For institutional investors, natural capital represents an opportunity to diversify portfolios, hedge against climate risks, and invest in sustainable environmental growth. The market needs scale, transparency, and integrity to attract large investment, and that's exactly what the Protector Profits Principle is designed to achieve.

By rewarding the stewards of our natural assets, we can create a pipeline of high-quality projects that offer predictable returns, measurable impacts, and opportunities for innovation. In this vision, conservation and investment go hand in hand. Institutional investors want stability and long-term prospects, and by aligning natural capital projects with these requirements, we open the door to billions in private sector capital.

The role of business leadership

In making the Protector Profits Principle a reality, the private sector must take the lead. The government isn't coming to save us, we cannot hope that regulation or philanthropy will drive the kind of change we need. Businesses, particularly those with significant land holdings or natural resource footprints, are uniquely positioned to make a difference. They have the capital, expertise, data, and networks needed to Scale Conservation efforts, but they need to see the financial benefit of doing so.

Leadership from the business community is crucial in setting standards, proving the profitability of natural capital, and building trust in these new markets. This means committing to radical transparency, sharing best practices, and being honest about the successes and challenges faced along the way. By setting a precedent and demonstrating real returns, early adopters can play a critical role in legitimising the natural capital market and encouraging others to invest.

Innovation and the green economy

Another benefit the Protector Profits Principle brings is fostering innovation. To meet the increasing demand for ecosystem services, we need new approaches, new technologies, and new business models. Whether it's advanced satellite technology to monitor biodiversity gains, blockchain to ensure transparency in credit trading, or agroforestry that combines productivity with ecosystem restoration, innovation will be key to scaling the impact of conservation.

Market-based solutions have always been effective at driving innovation. By creating a financial incentive for conservation, we are calling on the best minds and talents to find solutions that deliver both economic and environmental returns. The Protector Profits Principle unlocks the power of competition and creativity to solve the challenges we face, ensuring that the green economy is not just about compliance, but about growth, opportunity, and progress.

Critics will argue that monetising nature risks commodifying what should be protected for its intrinsic value. How's that going? The reality is that without a financial framework that recognises the value of nature, we will continue to see its degradation. The Protector Profits Principle represents a pragmatic path forward, one that acknowledges the need for economic incentives to drive meaningful change.

By making conservation profitable, we create an environment where market forces work in favour of, rather than against, nature. This is not about replacing regulation or abandoning the polluter pays principle; it is about adding another tool to the toolkit, one that rewards positive action and empowers those who are committed to stewardship, complemented by punitive measures critical for ensuring that those who harm the environment bear the cost. By combining these strategies, we build a comprehensive system that drives meaningful, long-lasting positive environmental impact.

The Protector Profits Principle is about reimagining the role of conservation in our economy. It's about ensuring that those who invest in protecting and enhancing our natural world are rewarded for their efforts – just as they would be for any other wise investment. By creating market mechanisms that align financial incentives with environmental outcomes, we can transform conservation from a cost to a cornerstone of our economic strategy.

We have a unique opportunity to create a market for natural capital that supports economic resilience, levels up rural communities, drives innovation, and attracts significant private-sector investment. By embracing the Protector Profits Principle, we can build a thriving nature-based economy – one in which protecting our environment is not only the right thing to do, but also the most profitable path forward.

It's time to lead the way, make the market for natural capital, and prove that conservation can drive prosperity, innovation, and sustainable growth. The world is ready. The opportunity is here. Let's make it happen.

On reflection

Reading this article back now, I'm struck by two frustrating things. First, how obvious this all is, and second, how far we still are from living it.

It's not radical to say polluters should pay. It's not outrageous to suggest that those who restore nature should profit. In fact, it's so painfully logical, it barely warrants explanation – and yet somehow, it's miles from reality.

That disconnect is infuriating. We have frameworks, we have science, we have models, and we have markets beginning to form, but the uptake? Minimal. The momentum? Fractured. The vision? Still seen as niche, idealistic, and even threatening to the status quo.

Here's the truth: the status quo is actively collapsing. Climate volatility is hitting agriculture hard. Biodiversity loss is accelerating. Rural communities are being gutted – not because of conservation, but because the current system no longer works. Everyone knows it. Everyone feels it. Yet still, change trickles when it should roar.

I wrote this piece not to state the obvious for its own sake, but to make it unavoidable. To put forward a future that aligns markets with morality, and pragmatism with purpose. While I still believe in that vision – deeply – I also recognise the courage it demands, because making this real means upending comfort, challenging legacy systems, and inviting a lot of people to think differently and criticise us along the way.

Yes, it's obvious. Yes, it's frustrating. It's also exactly the kind of thinking we need right now – simple truths delivered with honesty and relentless intent. If the world isn't ready for it, then we need to make it ready. Because we owe the future more than just good ideas – we owe it action.

ESG – The Label No Longer Relevant

Written October 2025

At the time of writing, the latest flurry of panic in the environment sector has related to Trump et al's impact on the ESG agenda. Are corporates abandoning ESG? Has the tide turned against sustainability? Before we leap to outrage or eulogies, let's ask a better question – are businesses really walking away from the commitments ESG represents, or are they simply outgrowing the label?

I don't think ESG is being rejected for what it stands for, but for what it has become – a label that no longer captures the depth, integration, or strategic necessity of sustainability today. Its moment as a standalone term may have passed, but was it ever meant to be a permanent fixture?

ESG was a provocation. A nudge. A bridge between the old model of blind shareholder/profit primacy and something better. Something that recognises that we cannot separate economic decisions from the systems they depend on: people, planet, and governance.

Bridges, however green, aren't for living on. They're for crossing. If ESG has done its job, if it has pushed corporates to consider consequences, nudged businesses to think longer, broader, more completely, then the fact we no longer need the label is not failure. It's evolution. It's proof that the idea worked. It's exactly what success looks like: integration so thorough it becomes invisible.

From label to logic

For years, ESG carved out a new way of thinking: that climate, nature, water, energy, soil, people, and governance aren't footnotes. They're foundations. It forced uncomfortable conversations in boardrooms. Launched many reporting regimes. Gave language to latent instincts. It helped map the messy middle ground between intention and implementation.

We said ESG made business sense. That it wasn't just ethical, it was smart. It would reduce risk, unlock new markets, attract better talent, and ensure long-term viability. If we meant that – really meant it – then it shouldn't be a badge anymore. It should just be what we do. We don't label companies 'digitally enabled' anymore. It's assumed. ESG should be too. Not as a siloed initiative, but as good business.

Every paradigm shift needs its moniker, until it doesn't. Quality Assurance in the 1960s, Total Quality Management in the 1970s, Lean Manufacturing in the 1980s, and Six Sigma in the 1990s, e-commerce and Corporate Social Responsibility in the 2000s, Social Media and Digital Strategy in the 2010s, and Digital Transformation and ESG in the 2020s. They were all useful when the ideas were fragile, but as they embedded, the labels started to feel performative, like pointing out that your car has seatbelts.

If we keep insisting ESG is special, we're tacitly admitting that sustainability is still optional. Still a nice-to-have. The real prize? When ESG stops being a differentiator because it's the baseline. When boards are embarrassed not to have the environment on their risk register. When investors simply expect integrated reporting to have considered ESG. This is what maturity looks like. Not louder claims, but quieter confidence. The logic becomes muscle memory.

Fear didn't fail, but it didn't inspire either

ESG's downfall wasn't due to irrelevance. It was a failure of narrative. Too often, it came wrapped in fear: climate catastrophe, ecosystem collapse, regulatory wrath. All true, but not exactly a rallying cry.

When ESG finally elbowed its way into capital markets, it did so through risk mitigation: compliance, litigation, and reputation management. Important, but uninspiring. It made sustainability feel like insurance, not innovation. Like a duty, not an opportunity, and opportunities are what fuel innovation and change.

It's time to pivot to opportunity

What's next? Ambition. Momentum. Imagination.

The new frontier isn't risk reduction, it's value creation. It's building the businesses that will power the regenerative economy. It's turning rivers into revenue, nature into balance sheet assets, and biodiversity into shareholder value. It's designing systems that are both high performance and high integrity.

Forget compliance. Let's talk competitiveness. Let's reframe ESG not as a burden, but as the beginning of competitive advantage. Not as a moral checklist, but as a strategy for building resilient, intelligent future-proof assets and enterprises.

There is a seismic shift happening under our feet. Natural capital is becoming one of the world's most important asset classes. Carbon credits are turning into investment-grade products. Ecosystem services are entering the mainstream of finance. This is not fringe anymore. This is the future.

What comes after ESG?

If ESG vanishes as a label, that might be the ultimate win. We'll know we've succeeded when ESG is no longer a thing. When doing business sustainably isn't noteworthy, but simply expected.

Let's not mourn the label. Let's bury it with honour. It got us this far. Now it's time to go further. Let's build companies where nature is a stakeholder. Where positive impact is a core strategy. Where sustainability isn't a side note – it's the operating system.

The label might fade, but the logic? That's not going anywhere; it's increasingly embedded.

On reflection

Sometimes I am accused of being overly optimistic. In this case, I hope not!

Why Profit Must Be Part of the Environmental Solution

Written October 2024

In discussions about environmental conservation, the notion of assigning a monetary value to nature often attracts criticism, with many feeling uncomfortable or that it's inappropriate. There's a prevailing sentiment that individuals and corporations should simply 'do the right thing' to protect the environment, or that investors ought to adopt a philanthropic approach, donating funds for the sake of conservation. While these arguments are rooted in a sense of morality, they overlook a fundamental reality: this isn't how the world works.

At the heart of the environmental debate lies a mistaken belief that business leaders, fund trustees, and investors can act purely out of altruism. The truth is, they legally and practically cannot ignore their financial responsibilities and fiduciary duties. Whether in the boardroom of a global corporation or the trustee meetings of a pension fund or charity, those in positions of financial stewardship are bound by duty – and often by law – to generate returns for stakeholders. However, we can and should now consider the planet a stakeholder.

Financial stability and success in business aren't and shouldn't be considered as inherently negative. They aren't adversaries of environmental progress; they are essential allies. Expecting the private sector to abandon the profit motive in favour of pure environmental altruism is an indulgence of fiction or fairy tale. While nature possesses a magical allure, our approach to saving it must be firmly grounded in the practicalities of economics and markets.

Public funds alone won't suffice

Another stark reality is that there isn't enough public money to address the environmental degradation we're all responsible for causing. Governments are financially stretched, and the challenges we face are immense and global. The imbalance is glaring: significantly more resources are funnelled into industries that harm the environment than can possibly reach those striving to protect it. The public purse simply cannot compete with the vast scale of private capital – it's an arms race that nature has lost.

If we desire real change, we must tap into the financial incentives that drive our modern world – you don't have to like it for it to be true. This means making it profitable to do the right thing for people and wildlife. Restricting environmental improvement to the realms of philanthropy or public funding is a limitation we can no longer afford.

Elevating environmental performance through profitability

We need to substantially raise the bar for environmental improvement, from funding mechanisms to execution strategies. Paradoxically, despite the moral criticism, embracing profitability is a crucial part of this elevation. We must create conditions where investing in sustainable practices is not only possible, but preferable and profitable. By making environmental restoration financially attractive, we can draw more capital, talent, performance, and innovation to the cause.

In a marketplace where investors constantly seek returns, environmental solutions must become more profitable than those of the industries causing harm. This is how we can shift the balance. If regenerating landscapes, restoring biodiversity, and building natural capital become compelling investment opportunities, the flow of money will begin to favour environmental solutions.

Overcoming internal divisions

A significant obstacle we face is the infighting within the environmental community – a kind of friendly fire that hampers progress. Too often, efforts are derailed by narrow focus and debates over whose vision of a better landscape is the 'correct' one – an example of this being those advocating for ground nesting birds over everything else in the landscape. In pursuing perfection (or often preference), we waste time, energy, and resources we don't have. Instead, we should unite behind a fundamental principle of progress: better is better.

We may not all, and almost certainly shouldn't, share the same vision of an ideal restored environment. Some may advocate for reforestation, others for rewilding, and still others for regenerative agriculture, but can we agree that any movement towards improvement – no matter how incremental – is preferable to inaction? By embracing iterative progress, we can achieve far more than by allowing perfection to be the enemy of progress.

The true moral imperative

Undeniably, there's a profound moral dimension to this issue. Critics assert that profiting from environmental improvement is unethical, believing that the sanctity of nature should remain untouched by commercial interests.

Let's scrutinise that stance. Is it not more objectionable to allow environmental degradation to persist simply because the solutions don't align with a purist non-profit ethos? By insisting that only altruistic efforts are morally acceptable, aren't we inadvertently endorsing inaction? Perhaps the greater ethical failing lies not in generating profit from healing the planet, but in letting it deteriorate because we refuse to harness the motivating power of financial incentives.

It is far more concerning when we fail to act than when someone benefits from doing good. The moral outrage should be directed at those who continue to exploit and harm the planet for profit – not at those who find ways to heal it while generating returns.

Ultimately, we must embrace the moral imperative to improve our environment. This moral compass must acknowledge that financial sustainability is a necessary component of any large-scale solution. Profit doesn't have to be the enemy of nature; it can be the reason for its regeneration and restoration.

This article draws inspiration from the classic episode 'The Moral Dimension' of the satirical series *Yes, Minister* (Jay and Lynn, 1982), where we are reminded of the complexities and ironies that often accompany moral decisions in the political and economic arenas. If you haven't watched the show, please do so, and quickly. In the episode, characters navigate the murky waters between ethical considerations and practical necessities, highlighting how rigid adherence to ideals can sometimes hinder effective action.

On reflection

Let's step into the conservation café for a moment. It smells like wet woodland and oat milk lattes. On the specials board? 'Altruism with a dash of nostalgia' and 'Philanthropic Pour-Over – bitter, beautiful, and completely unsustainable'.

At the corner table sits the idealist, sipping a long black and insisting that saving the planet shouldn't cost a penny or earn a pound. Meanwhile, the real action is happening at the counter, where the barista is pulling shots of reality: double espresso, no froth – full financial accountability.

'Why Profit Must Be Part of the Environmental Solution' was written with the intention of being the caffeine jolt conservation needs. I hoped it might shatter the comfortable illusion that good intentions alone will pay the bills, plant the trees, and rewet peatland bogs. You can't keep the lights on with moral virtue, and you certainly can't scale impact with a funding model that relies on guilt, grants, and goodwill.

Here's the brutal truth with a crema on top: money moves the world. It funds the pipelines and pesticides, yes, but it can just as powerfully fund the pollinators and the peatland restoration. If we want to win the conservation arms race, we need to compete not just on ethics, but on returns. We need to make rewilding more profitable than refining. Make tree planting sexier than deforestation and timber extraction, wetlands the new windfalls.

That doesn't mean selling out. It means brewing up a better model. One where the café isn't run on charity, but on sustainable cash flow. Where every flat white sold contributes to forest growth, and every investor sees biodiversity not as a box to tick, but a metric to multiply.

The real moral failure isn't that someone might profit from saving the planet – it's that we might let it die because we were too offended by the idea of profit to build a business case.

Order the flat white if you wish – but let's make sure it comes with a side of scalable conservation strategy. It's time to stop treating money like it's dirty and start using it to clean rivers, reintroduce species, and regenerate the landscapes we love.

In this café, profit isn't the problem – it's the power source.

THREE

The Trillion-Pound Opportunity: Profit With Purpose

Natural Capital: The Untapped Trillion-Pound Opportunity Hidden in Plain Sight

Written October 2024

Imagine a future where land – long seen as a static, utilitarian asset – is reimagined as a dynamic powerhouse that not only generates wealth, but also helps heal our planet and its people. This is not a utopian dream; it is the new reality being forged by natural capital investments.

However, this transformation isn't without its challenges. The road to creating a thriving natural capital economy is filled with obstacles, from securing substantial investments to navigating political volatility.

It is precisely in these challenges that the most extraordinary opportunity lies – a chance to be at the forefront of a movement that could become the next great revolution in real assets. Much like how technology reshaped communication and business, natural capital has the potential to transform our relationship with land and prosperity forever. The question isn't whether the opportunity is there – the question is who has the vision and courage to seize it.

Challenges

1. Investment

Investing in natural capital assets often requires a shift in mindset for traditional landowners and investors, as the returns tend to be long-term and not always immediately apparent. The challenge lies in developing financial models that clearly demonstrate how land-based natural capital projects, such as carbon credits or biodiversity offsets, can generate profitable returns.

Moreover, it is crucial to secure upfront capital for land acquisition and project implementation, which can be a barrier for many potential stakeholders. The significant scale of investment required, particularly for large restoration or ecosystem service projects, further raises the barrier to entry, making it difficult for smaller landowners or investors without substantial financial resources to participate meaningfully.

2. The environment sector

The environmental sector often operates in isolation from traditional profit-driven sectors. For landowners looking to engage in natural capital projects, there can be a lack of alignment between conservation objectives and the practical realities of managing land for financial return. The sector itself is relatively small, with projects generally being low value, slow-moving, and burdened by bureaucracy, which makes scaling initiatives challenging.

Compared to financial services, the environmental sector can lack the same level of professionalism, and the standard and work ethic may fall short of what is expected in more commercially oriented industries. Branding and marketing within the sector tend to be weak, which makes it difficult to attract investors and communicate the potential profitability of natural capital.

Furthermore, the talent base is limited, with fewer individuals possessing both the technical expertise and the commercial acumen necessary to drive forward impactful profit-oriented conservation projects. Bridging these gaps is essential to ensure that conservation efforts are economically viable and align with broader land management strategies.

3. Criticism

The concept of valuing natural assets and ecosystem services has faced criticism for commodifying nature, reducing it to a tradable asset. For landowners, this criticism can translate into reputational risks and backlash from stakeholders who believe that nature should not be exploited for profit.

Groups like No Farmers No Food have voiced concerns that natural capital projects may undermine traditional farming practices, potentially threatening food security and rural livelihoods. Similarly, sporting enthusiasts, who value land for recreational activities such as hunting and fishing, have raised concerns that monetising natural assets could restrict their access to these lands or lead to changes in land management that do not align with their interests.

Balancing the financial interests of landowners with the need to demonstrate genuine environmental stewardship is key to mitigating such criticism and addressing the concerns of diverse interest groups. However, achieving this balance can be challenging, as everyone's definition of environmental stewardship is different. This diversity of perspectives requires respectful consideration and the recognition that it's simply impossible to please everyone, especially when everyone thinks differently.

4. Technical challenges

This is incredibly complex.

Assessing and valuing natural capital assets on landholdings can be highly technical, requiring expertise in ecology, economics, and data analysis. For landowners seeking to monetise these assets, developing accurate valuations for biodiversity, carbon storage, or nature as a service is often complicated by a lack of standardised metrics and limited or poor data. This technical complexity can act as a barrier to entry for investors and landowners without the necessary expertise or access to reliable information.

Operationally, managing natural capital assets also presents significant challenges. Natural capital projects tend to require changes in land management practices, such as reforestation, wetland creation, or reduced grazing to replace traditional revenue-exploitation operations like intensive agriculture or commercial timber production.

For instance, large-scale tree-planting initiatives are labour-intensive and require careful species selection to ensure ecological compatibility and resilience. Similarly, controlling invasive species such as bracken, which can dominate the landscape, involves ongoing and costly management efforts. Deer management also poses a significant challenge, as unchecked populations can hinder reforestation efforts by browsing young saplings, requiring investment in fencing and culling to protect natural regeneration. These operational tasks are often resource-intensive and require specialised expertise, making it difficult for landowners to implement successful natural capital projects.

5. Communities

For landowners engaging in natural capital projects, navigating the expectations and interests of local communities can be challenging – it's often difficult to pinpoint who, in fact, identifies as local. Projects that focus on generating profit from natural capital may face opposition if communities feel excluded from the benefits or fear loss of traditional land-use practices. Moreover, community perspectives on natural capital projects can vary widely – some may support conservation efforts, while others prioritise farming, grazing, or sporting use. This diversity of perspectives can lead to conflicts over land use priorities, requiring careful negotiation to balance conservation and economic objectives.

There is also the potential for unreasonable community demands, such as full access to any and all land, insisting on their preferred land use (for land that they do not own), and financial compensation that may be unsustainable for the project. Managing these expectations requires transparent communication and establishing clear boundaries around what is feasible within the context of the project. Effective engagement and incorporating community needs into project plans are essential to secure local support, reduce conflict, and ensure that expectations align with the broader goals of the natural capital initiative.

6. Climate crisis

The unpredictability of the climate crisis presents a significant challenge for investment in natural capital. Land management decisions intended to enhance carbon sequestration or biodiversity could be compromised by climate-related impacts, such as wildfires or extreme weather events – we will see more of these! These risks add further uncertainty to the potential returns from natural capital projects, making it essential to adopt adaptive management practices that can respond to changing conditions.

7. Politics

Political uncertainty can also be a significant challenge for anyone looking to invest in natural capital, particularly given the early and volatile nature of carbon and BNG markets. Policies and incentives that support conservation and restoration efforts are often in flux, influenced by shifts in government priorities and changing regulatory landscapes. This volatility makes long-term planning difficult for investors and landowners who rely on the emerging carbon and BNG markets for returns.

The profitability of natural capital investments is closely tied to government subsidies, tax incentives, and regulatory frameworks that are still developing. As a result, any changes in politics or policy direction can lead to abrupt shifts in market conditions, affecting prices and demand for carbon credits or biodiversity offsets. This unpredictability makes it challenging for landowners to commit resources confidently, as the support mechanisms and market value they depend on may change without warning. Navigating these uncertainties requires a flexible approach, careful risk management, and staying informed about policy developments to adapt strategies accordingly.

The challenges of investing in natural capital, from securing significant upfront funds to navigating community dynamics and political volatility, are undoubtedly substantial. However, natural capital represents one of the biggest real asset opportunities the world has ever seen. This is a chance to redefine how we value and utilise our land, transforming it into a powerful force for ecological restoration and financial resilience. The early-stage nature of carbon and BNG markets means we are at the forefront of a movement that has the potential to reshape economies, create new revenue streams, and deliver significant environmental benefits.

Those who recognise and act on this opportunity now will play a pivotal role in creating a legacy of sustainable wealth and restored natural landscapes and see the potential for financial rewards.

Opportunities

1. Purpose

Natural capital investments provide a unique opportunity to align land – one of the oldest and most enduring forms of real asset – with a purpose-driven approach that maximises value across multiple dimensions: people, planet, and profitability. By monetising ecosystem services such as carbon credits, biodiversity improvements, or water management, landowners and investors can secure a stronger financial future while simultaneously contributing to environmental sustainability and community wellbeing. This approach elevates land beyond traditional use, turning it into an asset that supports ecological restoration, combats climate change, and enhances biodiversity.

Moreover, this dual-purpose strategy offers more than just financial returns; it delivers positive societal benefits that resonate with the growing demands of today's conscientious investors and consumers. By aligning investments with environmental and social goals, investors can significantly enhance their reputations, positioning themselves as pioneers in the emerging natural capital economy. This appeal is increasingly important in an investment landscape that is prioritising sustainability and impact-focused opportunities.

Ultimately, natural capital investments are not just about securing financial gains, but about creating lasting value that benefits all stakeholders – people, the environment, and future generations. This vision has the power to redefine the value of land and real assets in a way that ensures resilience and prosperity in an era defined by both opportunity and ecological need.

2. Talent

The growing interest in natural capital is attracting some of the most talented people across finance, ecology, and technology – individuals who are seeking not just a career, but a purpose-driven opportunity that goes beyond personal gain. These professionals are driven by the desire to contribute to something greater than themselves: to restore ecosystems, combat climate change, and make a lasting impact on the world. At the same time, they recognise the potential to do so profitably, aligning their values with financial success.

These people are breathtakingly talented – I know because I have the honour of working with a number of them!

This influx of passionate and capable individuals presents an incredible opportunity for investors to tap into a diverse and motivated talent pool that is eager to innovate and make a difference. These professionals bring fresh perspectives and creative solutions that can unlock new revenue streams from carbon credits, biodiversity offsets, and other ecosystem services, while simultaneously enhancing ecological health.

The enthusiasm and energy of these talented individuals are helping to transform the natural capital sector into a dynamic forward-thinking space, where profitability and positive environmental impact are no longer mutually exclusive. With the right talent, natural capital projects can not only meet financial goals, but also inspire a new generation of land management practices that benefit both people and the planet.

3. Scale

The scale of the market opportunity for natural capital investment in the UK is immense, with more than £20 billion worth of land and property identified as suitable for these types of projects. Landowning investors, especially those with large estates, are in a prime position to capitalise on this emerging market and unlock significant value through natural capital. By focusing on large-scale projects that restore ecosystems, sequester carbon, or enhance biodiversity, we can tap into premium opportunities in carbon and biodiversity markets.

The sheer scale of suitable land across the UK means there is potential for transformational impact – not just on individual estates, but on a national level. Leveraging economies of scale at the portfolio level allows landowners to maximise the efficiency of project implementation, lowering costs and boosting returns per acre. This approach creates the potential for substantial profitability, while simultaneously contributing to vital environmental and social outcomes, positioning natural capital investment as a highly attractive opportunity to make a real and measurable difference at scale.

4. Performance

The environment sector has a low performance bar, almost an innocent naivety, which presents an enormous opportunity for those committed to rapidly and effectively building a new real asset class. Just as the professionalisation of sport led to the creation of the Premier League and transformed rugby into being globally recognised, bringing a similar level of focus and professionalism to the natural capital sector can create transformative value. By raising standards, improving efficiency, and driving more strategic thinking, natural capital can become a high-performing, scalable investment opportunity.

5. Urgency

We don't have time to waste – we must act now!

The increasing urgency of addressing climate collapse and biodiversity loss has accelerated interest in natural capital projects, creating strong market demand for nature-based solutions. Investors and landowners can capitalise on this urgency by positioning their land as a source of valuable ecosystem services. As more businesses seek to offset their carbon footprints or invest in biodiversity, there is an urgent opportunity to meet this demand, generating returns and unparalleled positive environmental and social impact through strategic natural capital projects.

The convergence of purpose, talent, scale, performance, and urgency in the natural capital sector represents a rare and transformative moment in history – one where the ordinary can become extraordinary. Imagine the landscapes of the UK not as a static backdrop, but as dynamic, living real assets that create wealth, enrich communities, and rejuvenate the environment.

This is about more than investment; it is about rewriting the narrative of land and its potential.

As we stand on the brink of the greatest environmental and financial opportunity of our time, we have the chance to do what has never been done before: pioneer a new asset class that bridges human ambition with the needs of the planet. Just as technology has revolutionised communication and business, natural capital has the power to redefine how we value, interact with, and benefit from protecting the natural world.

For those bold enough to embrace this moment, the rewards are not only financial – they are nothing short of legacy-making. The question is not whether we can rise to this challenge, but who will seize the unprecedented opportunity to leave a lasting imprint on both the economy and the planet.

On reflection

When I wrote 'Natural Capital: The Untapped Trillion-Dollar Opportunity' in October 2024, it was still – just about – a provocation. A 'greenprint' for where we could go if capital, talent, and ambition aligned. Only a few months later, that future had already begun to materialise. The ideas are now no longer speculative – they're operational.

Institutional capital investors, once slow to engage with nature, are now stepping in with conviction. JP Morgan Asset Management recently (2025) launched a dedicated over $1 billion natural capital fund, investing in regenerative agriculture and ecosystem restoration across North America and Europe. AXA IM Alts has scaled up its natural capital strategy to target large-scale forestry and biodiversity offset projects, treating nature not as an abstract benefit, but as a bankable asset class (Tamssom and Mauvenu, 2025).

In the UK, Pollination and HSBC Asset Management continue to lead with their $1 billion Climate Asset Management platform (Thompson and Ford, 2024), which is already supporting UK-based woodland creation and peatland restoration. We're witnessing a surge of interest from pension funds and family offices seeking access to carbon-backed land portfolios – driven not by ESG box-ticking, but by clear, scalable financial incentives.

Why? Because the risks of inaction are now too costly to ignore – and the rewards for leading this shift are becoming too attractive to resist.

What I argued in 2024 – that land must evolve from a passive commodity into a regenerative engine of value – is exactly what we're now seeing in real-time. The rise of nature-based infrastructure funds, biodiversity credit pilots, and premium carbon credit markets proves one thing: the professionalisation of the sector is well underway.

Yes, many of the original challenges still remain. Complexity, community tension, and policy uncertainty are real, but they're being met with institutional-grade solutions: digital baselining tools, long-term land partnerships, impact verification standards, and legal mechanisms that didn't exist in 2024.

Natural capital is no longer an emerging idea. It is an emerging industry. What once sounded idealistic now looks inevitable. The question is no longer *if* this transformation will happen – it's who will be ready when it does.

Here we are, past the provocation, into the proof point. The trillion-dollar opportunity isn't hidden anymore.

Will Natural Capital Investment Mean the End of Philanthropy?

Written April 2025

People in the environment sector have been calling for private investment for decades, believing it to be the answer to their prayers. They think natural capital is coming to help them. It isn't.

This isn't salvation – it's a reckoning. Let me be clear: this is not a challenge, nor a criticism of the sector's incredible achievements. Instead, this is a warning given with love and kindness. We all owe so much to the wonderful people that created, led, helped, or donated to the Wildlife Trusts, Rivers Trust, Woodland Trust, National Trust and so many more beautiful organisations.

Those working in conservation NGOs and charities have dedicated their lives to protecting the natural world, often battling against insurmountable odds and painfully slow bureaucratic procedures. Their successes should be celebrated. Yet the future is shifting rapidly. The very thing they have invited – private investment – is both necessary and inevitable, but its consequences will be profound.

Natural capital markets are advancing, quietly but unstoppably, and people in the sector remain dangerously unprepared. The fundamental issue is clear: they seem to neither understand nor wish to understand the realities of investment.

When NGOs and charities talk about investment, they mean gifts, donations, and grants – a free-flowing stream of never-ending cash with no expectation of a return. It's a well-intentioned but fundamentally flawed approach. In reality, the sector has been hooked on philanthropy like a drug, utterly dependent and therefore resistant to change.

The toxic addiction to grants

Grants and donations have become the heroin of the environment sector, fostering a system where projects are shaped by funding cycles rather than the real, dynamic needs of nature and communities (of people and wildlife).

This slow, rigid formula fails to align with the urgency and unpredictability of ecological processes. The natural world doesn't operate on financial years, yet conservation organisations are forced to think in short-term one-off interventions dictated by the whims of donors or grant funding cycles.

The inefficiencies are staggering. The most talented people in the sector spend their time chasing grants instead of delivering meaningful environmental change. Rather than rewarding high performance and ambition, the sector is shackled by the fear of upsetting donors – we at Oxygen Conservation have seen it first hand with neighbouring landowners and partners sharing that they can't do what they know is right for the environment because of the fear that their donors won't like it. Innovation is stifled, all risk is avoided (at huge costs), and difficult decisions are dodged, delayed, or differed.

The addiction to grants and donations has not just shaped the sector's financial model – it has defined the way conservation is done. We're not standing outside throwing stones; we at Oxygen Conservation live and work in this system too. Some aspects of our work, from habitat restoration to species reintroduction, require grant funding to be financially viable in the current market.

This addiction isn't just bad for conservation – it's bad business. Actually, that's not fair; organisations locked in this cycle are not trying to be businesses. They can't scale, can't pay for the best talent, and can't break free from a perpetual dependency model. No industry thrives under such conditions, and the environment sector is no exception. Some of the most talented CEOs have managed to grow their organisations because they are exceptional at playing the funding game, but even they could achieve so much more in the private sector with the freedoms and tools that it brings.

Natural capital: The market-based future

There is an alternative: natural capital. The ability to generate a return from ecosystem services – whether through carbon sequestration, biodiversity credits, or developing these services – provides a way out of this trap, but it won't be the lifeline NGOs are expecting. It will first be a threat and ultimately a force that compels transformation. Some will evolve, while others may become obsolete.

With real investment comes the need for accountability, performance standards, impact measurement, and a market-rate return. Conservation will no longer be a charitable endeavour, but a financially viable industry – one that can attract institutional capital to scale effectively.

We have seen this transformation happen across countless industries, particularly in sports. Motor racing once existed as a pastime for passionate hobbyists tinkering in their garages, but today, it is a multi-billion-dollar industry led by Formula 1, where precision, data, and financial backing dictate success. Football, once an amateur pursuit played for the love of the game, has evolved into the Premier League and Champions League, global spectacles powered by strategic investment and high-performance management. Even cricket, steeped in tradition as a gentleman's afternoon pastime, has been revolutionised by the Indian Premier League (IPL), turning players into brands, teams into franchises, and the game into an economic powerhouse.

These examples illustrate the inevitable shift from passion-driven volunteerism to professional high-stakes enterprise. Conservation is no different. What was once the domain of well-meaning enthusiasts and charitable efforts is now evolving into a sophisticated investment-led industry. Those who continue to operate as hobbyists will find themselves left behind as the world moves towards structured performance-driven conservation that integrates financial markets, technology, and scalable impact. Just as sport has demonstrated, professionalism doesn't diminish the interest – it amplifies it, creating a space where ambition, talent, and strategic thinking can drive unprecedented success.

The rise of natural capital signals the end of many traditional environmental NGOs. Why would anyone donate money when they could invest it, earn a return, and reinvest in even more conservation work? The future belongs to organisations that can generate value, not just ask for it.

I recently sat down with Great Yellow's head of natural assets, Izzie Milligan, who highlighted the staggering number of environmental NGOs in the UK. She's right – the sector is fragmented, bloated, and often duplicative. As natural capital markets emerge, these inefficiencies will become increasingly untenable. The sector won't just need to adapt – it will need to survive.

Professional or amateur?

This is not about adaptation; it is about choice. Conservation as a professional, scalable business is emerging, and it will not wait for those unwilling to evolve. There will be a clear divide between those who embrace this transformation and those who remain trapped in the past.

The question is no longer whether conservation will become professionalised – it's already happening. The most talented people across the UK (and the world) are rushing towards the sector, and they are unreasonable, demanding, and incredible.

The real question is: do you want to be a professional, or will you remain an amateur? The days of well-meaning but financially naive conservation are numbered. The sector must decide if it wants to be part of the future or a relic of the past.

A future defined by bold action

Now the only decision left is how to meet this change.

To those who have dedicated their lives to conservation and fought for every acre of protected land and every restored river, this is not a dismissal of your work. This is a recognition that what got us here will not get us where we need to go. Passion is not enough. Grants are not enough. The planet does not operate on the timelines of funding cycles, nor can it wait for the slow drip of philanthropy to deliver the scale of restoration required.

The world is changing, and conservation must change with it. Those who seize this moment will not only protect and restore nature – they will redefine the very way we value it.

The future of conservation belongs to the bold, the strategic, and the relentless. It will be built by those who understand that impact and investment are no longer separate conversations, and those who can provide a meaningful return on both.

On reflection

Will the emergence of natural capital as an asset class mean the end of philanthropy for the environment sector? Yes, and so it should.

Green Returns: The Financial Upside of Woodland Creation

Written July 2024

In a world where tree planting is becoming ever more prioritised to combat climate change and the biodiversity crisis, we at Oxygen Conservation hope to see (and deliver) extensive areas of native broadleaf woodland re-establishing itself on marginal open hillsides. This vision of a greener, more biodiverse future is not just an environmental aspiration, but an incredible financial opportunity driven by the rapidly developing market for natural capital products and services. Investors are increasingly seeking high-quality carbon and nature credits as viable alternative assets.

The emergence of natural capital markets

The concept of natural capital involves recognising and quantifying the economic value of ecosystem services provided by natural environments. These services include carbon sequestration, biodiversity uplift, water purification, and recreational opportunities. By trading natural capital products and services, such as carbon and nature credits, investors can financially support the restoration and management of woodlands while earning returns on their investments.

Amenity woodlands, traditionally valued for their recreational and aesthetic appeal, are gaining new importance in the natural capital economy. These woodlands provide critical ecosystem services that can be monetised in various ways. For example, an acre of broadleaf woodland can sequester significant amounts of carbon, which can be converted into carbon credits and sold to companies seeking to offset their emissions.

Additionally, these woodlands can significantly enhance biodiversity, providing habitat for numerous species and contributing to the overall ecological health of an area. In time, they can also encourage access, enjoyment, and ecotourism opportunities.

Trading carbon and nature credits

The trading of carbon and nature credits represents a significant shift in how we fund and value natural landscapes. Carbon credits are generated by projects that reduce, remove, or avoid greenhouse gas emissions, such as reforestation. These credits can then be sold to companies looking to meet their carbon reduction targets. Similarly, nature credits can be created by projects that enhance biodiversity or restore ecosystems. Investors can buy these credits, thereby funding conservation efforts and earning a return as the value of the credits appreciates over time.

Value uplift through land transformation

One of the most compelling aspects of creating more woodland is the significant value in the uplift associated with the change in land use. Marginal bare hill land in Scotland, typically valued at around £1,250 per acre, can see its worth dramatically increase to between £3,000 and £5,000 per acre when transformed into amenity woodland (Priestley, 2024). This positive change in state not only enhances the ecological and aesthetic value of the land, but also represents a substantial financial gain. By creating more woodland, we are achieving a dual benefit: addressing environmental challenges while realising significant economic value from previously underutilised land.

Creating extensive woodland areas raises a valid question: will the increase in supply lead to a decrease in their value? While it might seem that an abundance of woodlands could dilute their worth, several factors suggest otherwise. Firstly, the demand for natural capital products and services, such as carbon and nature credits, is expected to rise significantly as companies and governments strive to meet stringent climate and biodiversity targets. This growing demand can offset the potential devaluation caused by increased supply.

Moreover, not all woodlands are created equal. High-quality, well-managed amenity woodlands that deliver substantial ecosystem services will continue to command a premium. The value of these woodlands lies not only in their physical presence, but in their capacity to provide ongoing benefits such as carbon sequestration, biodiversity enhancement, and recreational opportunities. As such, the emphasis should be on creating and maintaining woodlands offering high ecological and social value.

Additionally, the increasing recognition of the multiple benefits provided by woodlands – from improved mental health and wellbeing to enhanced ecosystem resilience – will likely sustain their value. Innovative financial instruments, such as green bonds and new impact investment products, will further support the economic viability of these projects.

Challenges and opportunities

However, this new model raises questions about the future value of amenity woodlands where natural capital products and services have been sold, and where management responsibilities are still present. One challenge is ensuring the long-term sustainability of these woodlands. Management practices must be adapted to maintain the ecological integrity and productivity of the woodlands while fulfilling the obligations associated with sold credits.

Another challenge is the need for robust verification and monitoring systems to ensure that the claimed benefits of carbon and nature credits are realised. This requires ongoing investment in technology and expertise to track and validate the performance of natural capital projects.

At Oxygen Conservation, our approach to these challenges is to never fully realise the value of any individual natural capital revenue stream without leaving sufficient funding within the project to cover all future potential responsibilities.

Future projections and trends for land value in a nature-based economy

With climate change raging across the globe and biodiversity challenges escalating, future trends point to a booming market for lands that deliver crucial ecosystem services like carbon capture, clean water, and positive benefits for people and wildlife.

As the climate crisis worsens, those once-overlooked patches of land are becoming home to an entirely new alternative asset class. This shift is driving up the value of amenity woodlands, catching the eye of investors and policymakers eager to harness nature's power to tackle environmental issues. Expect to see innovative financing like green bonds and new impact investment products making these projects even more appealing. Plus, tech advancements will make tracking and verifying ecosystem services simpler and easier, boosting investor confidence and making the valuation of natural capital assets efficient.

In short, land that helps buffer against climate impacts and boosts biodiversity will be in high demand, reshaping the market and highlighting the critical role of regenerative land management.

Seeing the wood for the trees

As we look ahead, the future of amenity woodlands in a nature-based economy opens up a wealth of possibilities and challenges. The potential of transforming underutilised land into thriving woodlands is immense, not just for the environment, but also for investors seeking sustainable and impactful opportunities. However, the journey towards realising this vision is complex and fraught with questions. How will we ensure the long-term sustainability of these woodlands while fulfilling our obligations to investors? Can we balance the increasing demand for natural capital products with the need to maintain high ecological and social value?

The answers to these questions are not straightforward, but they highlight the need for innovative thinking and robust management practices. As the market for natural capital products evolves, so too must our strategies for monitoring, verification, and long-term stewardship. The integration of technology, innovative financial instruments, and community involvement will be key to unlocking the full potential of amenity woodlands.

Ultimately, the future value of these woodlands lies in their ability to deliver a multitude of benefits – from carbon sequestration and biodiversity enhancement to improved mental health and community wellbeing. As we plant more trees and restore more landscapes, we are not just creating financial value, but also fostering a more resilient and sustainable world. The question remains: how will we rise to the challenge and seize the opportunity to reshape our economy and environment through the power of nature?

On reflection

Rereading 'Green Returns', I remain energised by the opportunity it outlines – transforming marginal land into thriving woodlands that deliver genuine ecological impact and meaningful financial returns. It's a vision I believe in deeply, and one we are actively building towards at Oxygen Conservation.

However, I'm the first to admit that this article continues to pose just as many questions as it answers. What happens after the credits are sold? Who holds the responsibility for future management when the ecology changes or challenges inevitably arise? How do we ensure robust, trustworthy verification of impact over decades, not just project cycles? How do we maintain the integrity of the woodland itself – ecologically and socially – especially as market interest accelerates?

These aren't abstract concerns. They are the hard practical questions we at Oxygen Conservation face every day in our work. While I'm proud of the steps we're taking – building long-term funding into every project, committing to rigorous monitoring, and striving for quality over quantity – I know we don't have all the answers yet.

I believe that amenity woodlands – even without carbon credits – will prove more valuable than barren sheep-wrecked hillsides or scorched former grouse moors, but short of inventing a time machine, I can't prove that... yet. Many of these challenges will take time to solve. They'll need collaboration across the entire natural capital economy – investors, landowners, tech providers, policymakers, and local communities. It won't be perfect, and it won't be fast, but that doesn't make it any less necessary.

The potential is huge, but so is the responsibility. It's in that tension – between ambition and accountability – that our work becomes most meaningful. It's a privilege to be doing this and to be doing it now.

Projecting Purpose: How the UK is Redefining Quality in the Voluntary Carbon Market

Written July 2025

The year 2023 was divisive for carbon credits, fracturing the developing market in two. In response to surging interest in the natural capital market from investors, Oxygen Conservation launched the UK's first forward pricing curve for high-quality carbon credits, the Stockdale-White Curve. However, while interest in the natural capital sector grew, 2023 also saw a series of high-profile controversies challenging the voluntary carbon market. The subsequent loss of trust in the market saw the value fall from $1.9 billion in 2022 to $0.7 billion in 2023 (Bennett, 2024).

The Stockdale-White Curve (the Curve) was developed out of necessity – a response to the persistent inertia within voluntary carbon markets and a deliberate step towards creating one of the tools required to make the market for natural capital. As environmental degradation accelerated and biodiversity declined, markets were stalling, stakeholders were hesitating, and institutional confidence was faltering. The credibility gap between global urgency and market action was growing untenably wide.

Our aim in developing the Curve was not to produce a flawless forecast, but to begin a discussion around the future of UK carbon prices and to build confidence in the investability of the market. We recognise that nobody can predict the future. We're all guessing, and we at Oxygen Conservation are clearly biased about the development of the natural capital economy. What the Curve aimed to provide was an initial approach to projecting carbon prices, one that generated a provocation grounded in both optimism and evidence, and ultimately clarified the investability and future scale of the UK's natural capital economy.

The Curve projected that the price of high-quality UK-based carbon credits would reach £60 by 2025, £150 by 2030, and a high point of £500 by 2050, making investment in UK nature-based solutions financially rewarding, unlocking significant volumes of private capital, and creating the UK's biggest alternative asset class, with the associated systems, processes, and intellectual property being the next big export for UK PLC. These estimates, considered bold at the time, are now increasingly credible. In 2025, the UK market witnessed a breakthrough £100/tonne of carbon transaction (Oxygen Conservation Carbon Curve, summer 2025), a valuation that exceeded our projections and reinforced our thesis that robust demand exists for high-quality verifiable credits that deliver genuine positive impact.

However, the Curve was never just about predicting prices. It was intended to be a catalyst for confidence and a statement of belief that investments in UK nature restoration can and should be financially attractive, provided they deliver meaningful environmental and social impact. Properly validated carbon credits can become a new form of climate currency, a true real asset class, one that restores trust, attracts institutional capital, and enables systemic environmental change.

Predictably, our model drew scrutiny. Some organisations adopted it as a pricing benchmark. Others criticised its assumptions. This is precisely what we intended. Challenging the status quo is essential in a field shaped by volatility, policy uncertainty, and fragmented data. Criticism and healthy debate drive refinement, and refinement builds resilience.

The 2025 Oxygen Conservation Carbon Curve

Eighteen months later (at the time of writing) and the Curve has evolved, including its name. As more people have joined us, bringing expertise, energy, and challenge, they've helped develop our thinking and push the curve into a new phase. That shift prompted a rebrand: the Oxygen Conservation Carbon Curve (the OC Curve). A name that better reflects both the collective effort behind it and the values that drive our work.

We updated and republished the Curve because the landscape has changed significantly. Emissions are still rising, but institutional actors are re-engaging with carbon markets. Integrity initiatives are gaining traction. The groundwork is being laid for nature-based solutions to enter mainstream asset allocation. Meanwhile, Oxygen Conservation has deployed over £125 million, acquiring 43,000+ acres to implement transformative restoration strategies across diverse UK geographies.

What the new OC Curve reflects is a fundamental divergence of the UK from the wider global carbon market. While the global market has seen a loss of trust, falling credibility, and declining volumes, the UK has seen steady growth year on year as buyers are drawn to its commitment to excellence. Within the UK market, we are also seeing fragmentation, as buyers increasingly pay to secure the highest quality and most impactful credits. The emergence of a new class of premium-quality credits is redefining what is possible in the carbon market and changing perceptions of what a carbon credit is.

We remain convinced that the UK can become the epicentre of a nature-based investment paradigm – akin to what Silicon Valley became for technology. The OC Curve is our signal to global markets: high-quality, transparent UK-based carbon credits have arrived, and they are investable at an institutional scale.

While we do not claim to predict the future with precision, we assert that shaping it is within our collective grasp. The OC Curve is not merely a speculative graph (or several) – it is a strategic framework, an intellectual invitation, and a rallying cry for capital to be directed towards regenerative outcomes.

This is more than a projection. It's a demarcation of intent. A visual articulation of belief in nature's financial, social, and ecological value, and a reminder that courage in forecasting can lead to courage in action. The OC Curve is our call to action – for investors to lead, for policymakers to enable, and for nature to win. It's time to move capital, shift norms, and back nature like our future depends on it – because it does. Let this be the decade we price carbon properly, fund restoration bravely, and finally, finally, make nature count.

On reflection

This reflection was written by the brilliant Peter Harker, partner at Saffery. His expertise in natural capital accounting made him the natural choice, not only to reflect on this article, but to shape both the Curve and the OC Curve from the start.

I'm genuinely honoured to have been asked to share some thoughts alongside this piece. All views here are my own – and when it comes to predicting future carbon prices, I'll almost certainly be wrong.

Clearly, both of the carbon curves Oxygen Conservation produced come with a degree of vested interest and potential bias. There are particular aspects which I myself have been critical of, but it's important not to dismiss them – they're a hugely valuable contribution. In a market starved of publicly available data, these curves give developers and investors something to work with. They create a common language for meaningful conversations, rather than leaving everyone guessing. Imperfect data beats no data every time.

The Woodland and Peatland Carbon Codes, with their Pending Issuance Units (PIUs), add an important ingredient to the considerations here. For businesses buying UK carbon credits as part of net zero plans, the logic often hinges on one big assumption: future carbon prices will rise faster than inflation and outperform other investments. In that light, a business purchasing PIUs is able to use such data as these curves to aid making informed risk-based decisions, effectively hedging against future costs.

Another important factor which the Oxygen Conservation Carbon Curve really draws out is the distinction that 'high-quality' schemes aren't just credits – they're stories, backed by assurance and transparency. That added value matters. It sets them apart from standard credits and gives businesses something more than just a tick in the carbon box.

Ultimately, only time will reveal how carbon is truly priced in the years ahead. What is clear, though, is that without businesses like Oxygen Conservation pushing the conversation forward and advocating for the sector, we risk carbon being treated as a commodity rather than a critical asset. That undervaluation would undermine both climate ambition and the credibility of net zero strategies – something none of us can afford to let happen.

FOUR

Rewilding Capital

Accelerating for Alpha: Why Speed is the New Strategy in Natural Capital

Written April 2025

One of the most profound – and necessary – shifts in the environmental sector is the rising value of speed. For decades, conservation moved at a pace that was, at best, patient and considered, and at worst, paralysingly slow. The process was deliberately methodical: think smaller, safer, steadier. When uncertain, have another meeting. Run a pilot. Delay the decision. Somehow, inertia became a feature rather than a flaw.

All the while, the climate deteriorated. Nature collapsed. Ecosystems grew quieter, less wild, and frighteningly less abundant.

Even today, some organisations still speak of their patience as though it's a virtue, a sign of credibility. In truth, it's become protectionist. It reinforces a closed elite system that too often resists real change.

However, something new is happening. As the crisis deepens, the environmental sector has opened its doors – often reluctantly – to the private sector. Calls for investment have grown louder, even desperate, but did we really understand what would come next?

Private capital doesn't just bring funding. It brings expectation, discipline, outcomes, and above all, *speed*. In a world where the planet is running out of time, where natural capital markets are maturing, and where returns – financial and ecological – are measured over time, we don't just need impact. We need the *rate* of impact.

This isn't slow conservation anymore. It's high-performance impact. Speed is no longer a threat to integrity – it's the only chance we have to keep pace with the problems we're trying to solve.

Lead with speed

At Oxygen Conservation, speed is not a tactic. It's a strategy. It's how we scale. It's how we lead.

Here's how we make it happen:

1. **Work ethic is contagious.** We don't worship burnout, but we do believe in working hard for something worth doing. The team works with intensity because we're driven by purpose, and surrounded by others who feel the same. That creates a perpetual improvement machine, producing ambition and accountability. We feel them in every interaction. This is not just a job – it's a mission, and it's addictive.
2. **Decision making as a trained skill.** We coach decision making like a sports team coaches strength and conditioning. We practise saying no fast and clearly. When we're hiring, if it's not a hell yes, it's a

no. Every day, we run our choices through the filter of our vision: does this get us closer to our goals? If not, we move on. No dithering. No indecision. Does that mean we make some mistakes? Of course, but we make them quickly.

3. **Talent.** We only hire people who are better than us. If we're not learning from someone in week one, we've made a hiring mistake. We invest heavily in recruitment and onboarding so every new hire lands at full speed. Great people don't need to be micromanaged – they need to be unleashed. That's how teams achieve incredible things.
4. **Transparency.** Speed hates secrets, so we default to openness. Whether it's internal metrics, land management strategy, or financial performance, we share more than most organisations would be comfortable with. This radical transparency empowers everyone in the business to act decisively and independently. There are no black boxes, no knowledge silos. There is no room for the slow creep of bureaucracy, or the cancer of the highest paid person's opinion.
5. **Diversity of thought = velocity of insight.** Homogeneous teams are comfortable, but dangerously slow. We intentionally construct teams with different backgrounds, lived experiences, and areas of expertise. In a sector often dominated by the same schools of thought (and frankly, the same schools), we believe that diverse perspectives are a strategic necessity. Diverse brains solve problems faster. They also have better debates and ask better questions earlier.
6. **Planning as a discipline.** Our calendars are detailed and shared. We plan a year ahead and

work backwards from impact. We don't let urgency become an excuse for being surprised by the obvious. Every project is sequenced for efficiency of delivery, with no dead time between steps. We build timelines like engineers (and yes, we have some of those on the team), not optimists (although we have some of those too).

7. **We build speed infrastructure.** Speed doesn't mean chaos – although we do love creative chaos sometimes. We systematise everything repeatable – from onboarding to reporting to tree planting. This isn't bureaucracy. This is what stops the team from wasting time reinventing the wheel. Every minute saved on routine is a minute gained for creativity and impact.
8. **Data.** Oxygen Conservation is a data company as much as it is a conservation business. From carbon baselining to biodiversity modelling to real-time land telemetry, our decisions are built on numbers, not gut instinct or romanticism. That's how we scale – by removing the guesswork and measuring what matters.
9. **Fail fast, learn faster.** Mistakes are fine. Sticking with them for months while hiding behind a Gantt chart is not. When something doesn't work, we kill it quickly and extract every lesson it has to offer. We treat failure like a data point, not a death sentence. There's no shame in a mistake – only in inertia, or repeating it.
10. **We don't like meetings.** Meetings slow us down. If something can be a shared doc or a message, it is. When we do meet, we come with decisions to make, not just status to update, and we cancel

anything that's no longer useful. Time is our most valuable currency – we spend it wisely.

11. **Elite partners as force multipliers.** We don't pretend to be experts in everything, so we surround ourselves with elite coaches – whether it's for legal, renewable energy, or woodland design. Like top athletes, we know that performance comes from specialised support. Our partners help us all work faster and deliver better outcomes.
12. **Iteration as an operating system.** We repeatedly ask: how can we go faster without falling over? We treat speed like a product – always iterating, always improving. We don't suffer the corporate disease of constantly adding new initiatives with marginal value. Simplicity is speed. Refinement is acceleration. Just like Formula 1, we believe in shedding weight to move faster. If it isn't adding value, we take it out.

Speed is the shift that changes everything

One of the biggest differences between the environmental sector of the past and the natural capital world of the future is this: speed matters now.

For too long, the sector has been gentle, comfortable, and proudly slow. Steady, methodical, consensus-driven. Watering down ambition into strategy papers and working groups. This cautious approach, once framed as wisdom, became self-serving. It protected legacy organisations and power structures. It built comfort, not change. While memberships swelled and budgets increased and/or quietly moved within civil service machinery to mask their real growth, the climate worsened and nature collapsed. Then, as the consequences became too big to ignore, the call went out for help from the private sector. For capital. For urgency.

The planet doesn't have time to wait, and neither do the investors funding its recovery. In the world we now inhabit, *rate of impact* matters just as much as impact itself. This isn't a world of Test cricket anymore. It's high-performance sport. It's the IPL (T20).

The point here is that as you shorten the game, you don't just accentuate the same skills more acutely, nor do you cause the same players to shift into different but similar modes. You fundamentally change the balance between and importance of different skillsets in interesting and unexpected ways.

The new era of conservation isn't slow, safe, or siloed. It's agile, transparent, and accountable. It's driven by data, talent, impact, and iteration. It's not about making a difference eventually – it's about making it *in time*.

We're playing a different game now, and we're playing it faster. That changes everything.

On reflection

What makes this shift towards speed feel even more significant is the arrival of AI. It has already collapsed timelines that once defined the environmental sector. Work that used to take months now takes minutes. Decisions that once depended on long chains of expertise can be tested, refined, and iterated in a single afternoon. AI has made acceleration unavoidable. It has turned speed from an aspiration into a default setting.

That truth was driven home for me during episode 101 of Oxygen Conservation's *Shoot Room Sessions* podcast, when we welcomed the godfather of sustainability himself, John

Elkington. With seventy-five years of experience behind him, he reminded me that in the age of AI, what once took ten years now takes two. Hearing that from someone who has witnessed every chapter of the environmental movement made it impossible to ignore just how quickly the ground is shifting beneath our feet.

Speed is no longer reckless. Slowness is no longer safe. The planet cannot wait, and neither can those building the systems that will restore it. AI is the most incredible tool. Our job now is to decide what is worth doing at this new pace, and to move towards it with intention, courage, and urgency.

Bridging Bytes and Biology: Comparing the Internet's Rise with Natural Capital Evolution

Written May 2024

At the confluence of two of the most significant challenges of our time, climate collapse and biodiversity crisis, the concept of natural capital – placing a monetary value on our ecosystems' resources – has the potential to be as revolutionary as the internet once was.

The technological evolution cycle describes the journey of a technology from its conception to widespread integration. It begins with the innovation stage, where visionaries conceptualise breakthroughs, often in academic or specialised settings. Next, the adoption phase sees these innovations tested and implemented in practical applications. This evolves into broader acceptance by the majority, leading to full-scale integration and, eventually, saturation within society.

Understanding this cycle provides an excellent framework to explore the parallel development of natural capital.

The genesis of the internet

The internet began as an ambitious concept in the 1960s with JCR Licklider's vision of an intergalactic network. This idea laid the groundwork for ARPANET, the first packet-switching network and the internet's precursor. Crucial developments such as TCP/IP protocols in 1983 and the domain name system in 1984 established the necessary infrastructure for global interconnection. These early stages were characterised by innovation and foundational groundwork, much like the changes we see today in the development of the nature-based economy.

Beyond the basic infrastructure, the internet saw rapid developments and enhancements. The introduction of commercial internet service providers (ISPs) in the early 1990s and the development of the World Wide Web by Tim Berners-Lee were pivotal. These advancements democratised the internet, moving it beyond government and academic domains to public and commercial use, leading to an explosion of growth and the dot-com boom.

Parallel paths: Natural capital's development

Just as the internet redefined communication, connectivity, and commerce, the emerging natural capital economy promises to reshape how we value, protect, and improve our natural environment. Understanding this transformation through the lens of the technological evolution cycle offers us unique insights into its potential trajectory and impact, as well as helping describe how very early we might be in the growth of a truly nature-based economy.

Discussions on ecological economics in the 1980s initiated the conceptual groundwork for natural capital. Influential works such as the Brundtland Report in 1987 (World Commission on Environment and Development, 1987) and the global dialogue sparked by the 1992 Rio Earth Summit laid early theoretical foundations, emphasising the importance of balancing economic growth with environmental preservation.

Infrastructure and initial adoption

By the mid-2000s, frameworks like the Millennium Ecosystem Assessment and initiatives such as The Economics of Ecosystems and Biodiversity (TEEB) began to quantify the economic benefits of biodiversity. The adoption of the Natural Capital Protocol in 2016 and the establishment of the Taskforce on Nature-related Financial Disclosures (TNFD) in 2023, following the Taskforce on Climate-related Financial Disclosures, represent the gradual but increasing application of these concepts within the finance and business sectors, mirroring the internet's move into commercialisation.

While we have the underlying infrastructure of the natural capital economy – our ecosystem itself – we have only just begun the process of building the economic, technological, financial, and regulatory systems we need. This includes the development of sophisticated environmental accounting systems that quantify and value natural capital, often supported by advances in geographic information systems (GIS) and remote sensing technologies that enable precise monitoring and management of natural resources.

Financial markets have begun adapting as well, with the emergence of green bonds and ecosystem service payments that incentivise conservation and sustainable practices. Policy frameworks and regulatory bodies are also evolving to support this shift, setting standards and guidelines that ensure environmental impacts are considered in economic activities. Additionally, numerous global initiatives and partnerships have become established to promote knowledge sharing, capacity building, and financial investment in natural capital projects, illustrating a broad-based commitment to integrating ecological health into the global economy.

Challenges and scaling up

The development and adaptation of nature-based economic principles is incredibly difficult. Many businesses are still learning how to integrate ecosystem services into their financial calculations. Moreover, the regulatory environment is evolving, which adds a layer of complexity to valuation and reporting.

For example, in the UK, we have only just received information on how HMRC will treat carbon credits from a VAT perspective (May 2024). So many questions remain unanswered, and there are many more we haven't even thought to ask. These challenges are reminiscent of the early days of internet security, systems, structures, and processes, all needed ahead of things like data laws and regulations, where standards had to be established to monitor growth and foster trust.

Readying for adaption

While a few pioneering organisations are stepping into the adoption phase of natural capital, the majority are still deeply entrenched in the innovation and infrastructure-building stages. Much like the early days of the internet, where initial developments were focused on establishing foundational technologies and protocols, the natural capital economy is currently laying down its own critical groundwork.

Organisations like the Foresight Sustainable Forestry Company, Federated Hermes, and Finance Earth (and so many more since this was first written) are at the forefront, integrating natural capital into their strategic frameworks. However, akin to the nascent internet era, marked by a landscape of experimental technologies and emerging standards, the field of natural capital is characterised by a high degree of innovation with an ongoing need to develop the infrastructure and fundamental principles necessary for broader economic integration.

The challenges ahead are fiendishly difficult. Much of the detailed mapping of this new terrain is yet to be undertaken. Businesses and governments are still grappling with how to effectively integrate ecosystem services into economic planning, regulatory frameworks, land use policy, and corporate strategies.

The evolution of the regulatory landscape (in every sense of the word) is especially important when we're adding layers of complexity to an already intricate valuation and reporting system. These hurdles mirror the early obstacles faced by internet pioneers, who had to establish security protocols, user trust, and regulatory compliance in a world not afforded the connectivity or access to information we ironically enjoy as a result of their work.

Despite these challenges, the trajectory of natural capital and the nature-based economy is clear. Just as the internet grew from a collection of isolated networks to become the backbone of global infrastructure, so too does natural capital hold the potential to transform our economic landscape. By learning from the technological evolution of the internet – recognising the importance of early innovation, the gradual shift to adoption, and the critical role of infrastructure – we can better prepare for the next stages of growth in the natural capital economy.

As we stand at this crossroads, it is crucial to continue fostering an environment that encourages exploration, supports innovation, and ultimately facilitates the widespread adoption of natural capital principles. With sustained effort and strategic foresight, we can ensure that the valuation of our natural resources evolves from a fringe concept into a central pillar of sustainable economic development.

The journey is long, and much remains to be done, but the path forward is promising. For all of you out there working so incredibly hard to make the natural capital economy a reality, please keep going, but remember it's OK to take a moment, recognise how far we've come, and understand we have an incredibly long way to go!

In the world of the internet, we're in the mid-1990s. We're all using AOL, Yahoo! is the most exciting company on the planet, Amazon has just started selling books, and eBay has not yet launched. Oh, and the first iPhone is a decade away; Steve Jobs has just returned to Apple. Imagine what the next twenty years of the natural capital economy will bring. We're fortunate to be on this journey and I'm so excited to be playing a part in building the future.

On reflection

When I look back at this piece, written in May 2024, it feels like opening an early-stage prototype of an idea that has since accelerated faster than any of us could have predicted. At the time of writing, we were still guessing at regulatory frameworks, debating valuation models, and trying to convince people that natural capital wasn't just a fringe thought experiment borrowed from ecological economics. Now, reading the article again with the benefit of knowing everything that has happened since, I'm struck by how quickly this field is maturing, how rapidly the conversation is shifting, and how early we still are in its evolution.

This article is one I return to often, because it has a strange quality: it keeps updating itself as the world changes. Every time AI leaps forward, every time new guidance drops from TNFD, every time a major institution adopts natural capital accounting or an entirely new market emerges, the analogy grows sharper. It doesn't just hold up. It becomes more true.

What began as a comparison between the early internet and the early natural capital economy now feels like a roadmap. The 2024 version of me wrote it at the moment when natural capital was still booting up: pre-revenue models in many places, early adopters experimenting in pockets, regulatory frameworks flickering into life. Today, as I revisit it, we are already several software updates later. The valuation mechanisms are improving. The data pipelines are strengthening. Investors are becoming more sophisticated. The scale of opportunity has grown from ambitious to inevitable.

Natural capital is no longer the shy sibling of tech. It has become a parallel internet of living systems: a network of habitats and processes where carbon, biodiversity, water, and soil are the packets and protocols of a new ecological infrastructure. If the internet connected us to each other, natural capital might just reconnect us to the planet itself.

We are not at the dot-com boom of nature yet, but we are certainly beyond dial-up. The AOL-era version of natural capital described in this article has evolved into something closer to broadband. Our Taskforce on Nature-related Financial Disclosures (TNFD), Biodiversity Net Gain (BGN), Monitoring, Reporting and Verification (MRV) platforms, and carbon markets are the TCP/IP of a fast-emerging eco-economy, and the innovations coming next will make today's breakthroughs look quaint.

That's why this piece remains so important to me. It wasn't written to be definitive. It was written to be iterative. To ask the right questions at a time when almost nobody was asking them. To imagine what a functioning nature-based global economy could become if we committed to building it with clarity, courage, and scientific integrity.

Now, with the benefit of distance, what strikes me most is not the comparison to the internet, but the invitation the article extended to think bigger. To be early. To be unreasonable. To help engineer the operating system that will stitch together ecology, finance, land management, and technology in ways we are only beginning to understand.

Let's keep going. Keep debugging. Keep upgrading. Nature 2.0 is still loading, but far faster now than when these words were first written, and I am extraordinarily fortunate to be part of the team prompting AI to write the code.

Zero to Nature: Why Oxygen Conservation is Building the Future of Environmental Investment

Written October 2025

Peter Thiel is a renowned entrepreneur, investor, and author whose insights have shaped the trajectory of some of the world's most transformative companies. A co-founder of PayPal and Palantir, and the first outside investor in Facebook, Thiel has a contrarian approach and deep understanding of technology and markets that have made him a guiding force for a generation of founders. His book *Zero to One* (2015) introduced the Thielian Tests – seven questions that probe whether a business can be truly transformative, not just another player in the market. These questions are now a rigorous framework for evaluating the potential of any ambitious venture.

At Oxygen Conservation, we are redefining conservation as a high-performance data-driven enterprise that delivers environmental, social, and financial returns. Our approach challenges conventional sustainability and actively builds a future where ecological and economic resilience are inseparable.

Here's how we answer each of the Thielian Tests.

1. The engineering question: Can you create a breakthrough technology instead of incremental improvements?

Oxygen Conservation is not in the business of marginal gains. We are committed to creative destruction – dismantling outdated models of conservation and rebuilding them for a world that demands both pace and performance. Our proprietary data acquisition model is at the heart of this transformation. We harness a vast array of environmental and economic data to rapidly determine natural capital potential and value at scale.

Our custom tools include a screening model that analyses spatial data layers and runs multiple financial simulations for every landscape under consideration. This enables us to make informed decisions quickly and efficiently, ensuring that we acquire the most suitable places and spaces for Scaling Conservation.

Beyond acquisition, we have developed sophisticated techniques for asset management and running estates. Our use of automation tools allows us to build geoprocessing workflows for evaluating land parcels and gathering data to inform investment decisions. Each site is equipped with a custom web application – an interactive data viewer – enabling the team and our stakeholders to access real-time information on habitats, biodiversity, water quality, and more. This system is not just an improvement; it is a fundamental reimagining of how conservation assets are evaluated, acquired, and managed.

2. The timing question: Is now the right time to start your particular business?

There has never been a more important time to build a business like Oxygen Conservation. Climate change and biodiversity loss are not distant threats; they are present-day realities. The world is waking up to the value of natural capital, with nature-based solutions moving from the margins to the mainstream. Policy frameworks are evolving to support ecosystem valuation, and the appetite for private investment in nature is growing rapidly.

We were not the first mover in the sector, but we were very early. We learned from those who went before us, accelerating quickly to take a leading market-making position. Our early entry allowed us to shape the sector's standards, metrics, and ambitions.

With this position comes responsibility: we are committed to championing everyone in the sector, sharing our learnings and helping to build a robust, high-integrity market for natural capital. The convergence of environmental urgency, economic demand, and regulatory support makes this a once-in-a-generation opportunity. It's not just us that think that – the Secretary of State for Net Zero used those exact words before our keynote announcement of a new world record price for nature-based carbon credits during London Climate Action Week 2025.

3. The monopoly question: Are you starting with a big share of a small market?

Oxygen Conservation holds the first institutional-scale land portfolio in the UK natural capital sector. This is a platform for continued growth and influence. At the time of writing, our holdings exceed 50,000 acres, connecting over 500,000 acres through partnerships and adjacent initiatives. In a sector still defining itself, we are the operational and ideological frontrunner.

This is just the beginning. We estimate the UK's natural capital acquisition potential at nearly £20 billion over the next decade, with a finance gap for nature-related outcomes between £44 billion and £97 billion over ten years.

The appetite for investment in climate and nature is enormous, and globally, the figures are even more astonishing – natural capital assets under management worldwide are valued at around £200 billion, with rapid growth expected as markets mature (2024-2025). Our vertically integrated model, spanning land acquisition, asset management, habitat restoration, credit generation, and storytelling, gives us end-to-end control and a first-scale-mover advantage in a market poised for exponential expansion.

4. The people question: Do you have the right team?

The Oxygen Conservation team is our greatest asset, not in the same tired, constantly trumpeted corporate way, but in a genuinely heartfelt, meaningful way. They are the powertrain that drives our ambition. We've cultivated a culture that draws exceptional individuals from far beyond the traditional boundaries of conservation. Our recruitment playbook is inspired by elite sport: we scout for raw talent, potential, and passion – not just CVs.

We've attracted thousands of applicants, particularly young professionals who might never have considered conservation as a career path. They're drawn by the purpose, yes – but also by the pace, the culture, and the opportunity to do something that matters. Our team includes ecologists, data scientists, economists, filmmakers, estate managers, and strategists – all united by shared values: high performance, relentless curiosity, and a deep sense of responsibility.

This is not just a team. It's a movement. A culture. A living, evolving expression of what conservation can become when you bring the right people together and give them room to lead.

5. The distribution question: Do you have a way to not just create but deliver your product?

We own our distribution from start to finish. Every product – whether a carbon credit, biodiversity unit, or educational experience – is delivered with the care and professionalism of a luxury brand. Delivery for us is not just logistics; it's narrative. Our distribution strategy is built on premium personalised relationships and brought to life through a robust multi-channel communication ecosystem.

We've created a powerful media engine to reach, educate, and engage our audiences – from global investors to local landowners. This includes our *Shoot Room Sessions* podcast, where we discuss the challenges and opportunities of conservation with industry leaders. Our growing library of books, long-form essays, and written thought leadership helps to establish intellectual credibility. Our digital media – videos, social channels, newsletters – reach thousands and build community (digital and physical).

These communication platforms have helped us forge transformative partnerships with values-aligned institutions such as Triodos Bank, Knight Frank, Burges Salmon, and Low Carbon. These partners are not just collaborators; they are champions and multipliers of our mission. They help expand our distribution capacity – whether by unlocking capital, structuring deals, navigating legal landscapes, or scaling clean energy solutions.

6. The durability question: Will your market position be defensible ten and twenty years into the future?

We're thinking about our impact for the next 100 years!

Every project we design, whether it's restoring ancient woodlands, rewetting peatlands, or generating premium carbon credits, is rooted in the principle of permanence. Our horizon is a century long. Our legal agreements reflect this; they're robust, binding, and built for legacy. We don't just think long-term; we integrate permanence into the roots and branches of everything we do.

By owning the land we acquire, we lock in control and unlock accountability. This means we can make generational decisions rather than transactional ones, and it means our position gets stronger – not weaker – with every passing year. Each estate restored, each ecosystem revived, adds to a flywheel that's already spinning faster than anyone else's.

We seek to hard code permanence into every project. Our independent management team is empowered to make bold decisions, free from short-term pressures but deeply aligned with long-term investor value. We've built a culture of high performance and innovation that constantly evolves – developing geospatial tools, redefining estate management, and shaping a new language for nature.

This is not a trend. It's a transformation.

In a world where nature-based solutions are increasingly seen as essential infrastructure, our integrated model – combining land ownership, carbon and biodiversity credits, renewable energy, sustainable agriculture, ecotourism, and community engagement – is uniquely resilient. Durability isn't an ambition – it's something we've designed, built on land, backed by law, and strengthened by time. It's designed not just to withstand the next two decades, but to shape the next century.

7. The secret question: Have you identified a unique opportunity that others don't see?

The secret is simple, but radical: conservation doesn't have to be charity. It can – and must – be investment. The belief that nature should always be a cost rather than a contributor belongs to the past. We at Oxygen Conservation recognised early on that with the right structure, landscapes could become viable, scalable, investable assets, and we built the model to prove it.

This model values nature not just for its beauty, but for its potential to store carbon, regenerate biodiversity, deliver renewable energy, support homes and rural jobs, and offer strong financial returns. This is ecosystem regeneration reimagined as a high-integrity asset class, and we're laying the operational, digital, and financial infrastructure to bring it into the mainstream.

That's just the beginning. We understand that stories are infrastructure too. That a podcast can spark trust. A book can mobilise a movement. That telling the story of a place can be as powerful as planting a tree within it. At Oxygen Conservation, we've built the channels – *Shoot Room Sessions*, digital media, long-form writing – to do just that.

Scaling Conservation

Oxygen Conservation is not simply another voice in the environmental sector. We are architects of a new natural capital economy. We don't just meet Peter Thiel's seven criteria; we stretch them, challenge them, and build on them. Our model proves that conservation can be high-performance, high-integrity, and high-impact. For those in sustainability, finance, or environmental governance, Oxygen Conservation is more than a case study – it's a blueprint for how vision, data, and determination can create lasting scalable change.

We are not finished. We are not even close, but we are moving. Fast.

The future of conservation is not about waiting for permission. It is about building the future we want to see, with the tools, the talent, and the tenacity to make it real.

If Peter Thiel ever stumbles upon this manifesto, we at Oxygen Conservation hope he sees not just a nod to *Zero to One*, but its living, breathing evolution – built in soil, sung by birds, and scaled through purpose. Perhaps one day soon, he might even feel compelled to shift capital from code to carbon, from Palantir to peatlands and Silicon Valley to actual valleys.

On reflection

Some people didn't like that I referenced Peter Thiel when this piece was first released. He is a divisive figure, and invoking his work brings all the complexity, discomfort, and contradiction that comes with him, but that reaction is exactly the point I keep returning to: if we only allow ourselves to learn from those who make us feel safe, we shrink the intellectual territory we can operate in. We start optimising for approval rather than impact, and in a world where nature is collapsing in real time, that is a luxury we simply do not have.

I didn't reference Thiel because I agree with every view he holds. I referenced him because his questions are sharp, useful, and uncompromising – and because building a new asset class requires tools forged outside the environmental comfort zone. The sector is full of brilliant, well-intentioned people, but it can also lean towards homogeneity, towards talking only to itself, towards mistaking moral alignment for strategic clarity. If we want to Scale Conservation at the pace the planet demands, we need to be willing to cross intellectual boundaries, borrow good ideas from unlikely places, and sit with the discomfort that follows.

Some people didn't like it. That's fine. Progress rarely comes with unanimous applause. What matters is whether the ideas help us restore more ecosystems, attract more capital, and accelerate the regeneration of the landscapes we are responsible for damaging.

If a question first posed in Silicon Valley helps us heal a peatland in Scotland or a river in Wales, then I'll take the criticism – and keep asking the questions. Oh, and without Silicon Valley there would be no Oxygen Conservation.

Compounding Conservation: How We're Building the World's First Conservation-Focused Unicorn Company

Written July 2025

Oxygen Conservation doesn't resemble traditional conservation companies, and this is by design. From day one, we set out to build something fundamentally different: a business model capable of sustaining itself, scaling aggressively, and making generational impact. This isn't about fitting into an existing mould. It's redefining conservation.

We've fused together an elite performance culture with bold branding, advanced data science, strategic land management, systems-level engineering, and a clear investment thesis to redefine what conservation can be in the twenty-first century. Our ambition is to create an entire new sector – structurally, culturally, and economically. This is the conservation equivalent of building the next Google or SpaceX: vision-led, ruthlessly executional, and unafraid to rethink the fundamentals, and we're doing it on the foundation of five deeply integrated, radically ambitious principles.

1. Talent

We've attracted and assembled the very best talent – individuals with the kind of ambition, creativity, and capability the conservation sector has never been able to secure before. We won't peak for at least another decade. What we've built is a generational force capable of delivering remarkable achievements year after year. This team isn't here to maintain. It's here to dominate.

Oxygen Conservation is intentionally building the highest-performing team in the natural capital sector. Inspired by elite athletic training, our people strategy focuses on identifying high-potential individuals, developing their skills rapidly, and aligning their personal growth with our broader mission.

We do not settle for adequate – we hire individuals with the capacity to grow beyond their role. From the beginning, our intern programme has served as an incubator for future leaders, and our estate teams function as interdisciplinary units focused on execution and impact. As our organisation expands, we invest in people who challenge conventional thinking and raise the performance bar for everyone.

We recruit talent from diverse sectors – finance, technology, environmental science, and creative industries – because cross-pollination of ideas leads to innovation. Our culture values proactive learning, direct feedback, and continual evolution, all supported by clear performance expectations. Our aim is to grow our team and, at the same time, elevate the entire sector by setting a new standard for what environmental professionals can be.

2. Technology

One of our biggest advantages is the proprietary technology we're developing in-house. Rather than relying on outdated, fragmented systems, we're building digital tools specifically designed to evaluate, manage, and enhance the value of natural capital at scale.

Our proprietary, confidential technology allows us to:

- Model the financial value of ecosystem services like carbon sequestration and biodiversity uplift with unparalleled speed and accuracy
- Integrate diverse datasets to monitor ecological change in real-time
- Operate complex large-scale land portfolios with high precision and accountability
- Continuously improve with every data point: each new ecological or financial insight feeds into a perpetual learning machine – refining our valuation models, restoration strategies, and investment decisions in real-time

This infrastructure transforms conservation from an anecdotal science into a rigorous, measurable, and investable enterprise. It also creates a competitive moat: as we continue to innovate, our insights and decision-making processes become faster, more accurate, and harder to replicate.

3. Network effects

Nature thrives in interconnected systems – and so do we. Every new estate added to our portfolio enhances biodiversity, boosts carbon sequestration potential, and increases landscape-scale resilience, but the ripple effects go much further. Each acquisition amplifies our capacity, data intelligence, and stakeholder trust. It's a compounding engine of ecological and strategic value.

Network effects also power our human infrastructure. As we attract more investors, scientists, creatives, and policymakers, the entire natural capital ecosystem accelerates. New entrants bring new ideas. New ideas spawn new ventures. More capital, more awareness, and more collaboration create the conditions for spin-out startups, novel services, and next-gen environmental finance products.

Natural capital is no longer a static asset. It's a networked asset platform – interdependent, dynamic, and exponential in its potential. As each node strengthens, the whole system grows more robust. This is why we're not just scaling landholdings – we're scaling the sector, and in doing so, we're building the infrastructure of a regenerative economy.

4. Economies of scale

Conservation projects often remain small because they lack the necessary ambition, investment, professionalism, and infrastructure to expand. Oxygen Conservation was designed to solve that problem from the outset. We've built an elite central team – market-defining in its capability and culture – paired with agile place-based estate teams that deliver operational excellence at the local level. This model enables us to deploy scalable strategies across more than 50,000 acres without sacrificing quality or integrity.

We also benefit from proprietary data, systems, and processes that drive efficiencies in every part of the business – from land acquisition to project delivery, monitoring, and reporting. These tools empower us to move faster, make better decisions, and optimise resource allocation across an ever-growing portfolio.

Beyond our internal infrastructure, we've cultivated an exceptional network of specialists – ecologists, foresters, community leaders, and contractors – who enhance our site-level understanding and delivery capacity. They are an extension of our team, ensuring local knowledge and relationships are integrated into every project. The result is a true economy of scale: with every new acquisition, the marginal cost of delivery decreases, operational efficiency improves, and our capacity to deliver high-impact projects grows. All without diluting standards or compromising integrity.

With our first portfolio nearing maturity, we plan to bring it to market and use the capital generated to seed Portfolio Two. This reinvestment model – where capital flows directly into new land acquisitions and restoration efforts – is designed to rapidly scale our assets under management and push towards a target of £1 billion worth of assets under management (AUM). It's a regenerative investment cycle that delivers financial, environmental, and social returns year after year.

5. Brand

Conservation has too often been trapped in a narrative of gentleness and charity – well-meaning, but not world-changing. We exist to change that perception and to set a new standard.

Oxygen Conservation has built a brand that is unapologetically ambitious. It's not just visible – it's magnetic. We've created a platform that attracts the most talented individuals and the most discerning institutional investors because it reflects clarity, confidence, and purpose. Our brand tells the story of what's possible when high-performance culture meets deep environmental commitment.

We've declined investment when it conflicted with our values. Not as a marketing tactic – but because our integrity is non-negotiable. Our brand is not a veneer – it is the external reflection of an internal discipline. It's built on truth, on results, and on the confidence to lead where others follow.

From podcasts and publications to policies and portfolios, our voice is consistent, credible, and catalytic. It allows us to influence public opinion, shape national conversations, and define new standards in a nascent but rapidly growing sector.

Our brand is our gravity. It pulls talent, capital, and opportunity into our orbit. More than that, it projects a vision of conservation as something bold, investable, and scalable. A vision capable of inspiring the next generation to see this work not as a sacrifice, but as a career of consequence.

On reflection

At Oxygen Conservation, our advantage is the compounding impact of strong foundations: elite talent, cutting-edge technology, systemic networks, scalable strategy, and a completely authentic mission-driven brand. These aren't just assets. They're accelerants.

This is why Oxygen Conservation is a business that's accelerating – scaling both impact and profitability simultaneously. We are becoming more valuable with every acre bought and restored, every credit issued, every job created, and every story shared. By 2030, we will be a unicorn. This will be a validation that conservation done differently is not only investable, but unstoppable.

Everything compounds!

A Unique Vintage

Written March 2025

In the developing world of sustainable investments, premium quality carbon credits and natural capital products and services are emerging as compelling opportunities for investors and corporate buyers alike. They have the potential to generate significant returns while contributing to tackling the twin crises of climate change and biodiversity loss.

At the time of writing, Oxygen Conservation was uncorking a new standard for natural capital products in the UK. Our 2024 vintage of carbon credits represents the 'grand cru', a landmark opportunity for those who recognise the important role that premium quality carbon credits can play in their net zero strategy.

The premium appeal of vintage carbon credits

Much like a prized cuvée, vintage carbon credits offer an unparalleled combination of quality, provenance, and exclusivity. Each of Oxygen Conservation's 2024 vintage credits is the result of meticulously crafted ecological restoration projects, maturing in some of the UK's most cherished landscapes. This vintage is singular in nature – our 'prestige reserve'.

As the global race towards net zero accelerates, the demand for high-quality carbon credits has effervesced, akin to a finely aged champagne in a celebratory glass. Businesses and governments are embracing these premium credits to align with their ESG goals, providing investors with the dual opportunity of financial return and a toast-worthy impact on environmental and social progress.

Oxygen Conservation's 2024 vintage explained

1. Measurable ecological co-benefits

Unlike many other credits, Oxygen Conservation's carbon credits are generated from projects delivering a symphony of environmental enhancements on land we own and manage for conservation. From the restoration of temperate rainforests to the planting of new broadleaf native woodland, our credits sequester carbon while improving biodiversity, enhancing water quality, and mitigating flood risk.

2. Transparency and trust

Each credit is fully traceable to its source project and underlying natural capital asset, with detailed data on its environmental and social impact provided through annual reports. Our partners are encouraged to visit each project to touch, feel, and connect with the positive impact they're having on the natural world – to experience the 'terroir' first hand. This radical transparency instils confidence and ensures that buyers can demonstrate progress against their sustainability commitments.

3. Market-leading standards

Our credits adhere to the highest protocols and use cutting-edge technology to provide a digital monitoring, reporting, and verification system which records landscape changes at centimetre-level precision. This ensures durability, permanence, and additionality – key factors informed buyers prioritise. Each credit also provides a range of co-benefits to people and the environment, making measurable contributions to nine of the United Nations Sustainable Development Goals and providing tangible contributions to corporate ESG strategies.

4. The Stockdale-Winter Carbon Curve: value on the rise

A cornerstone of the 2024 vintage's investment appeal lies in its sparkling position on the Stockdale-Winter Carbon Curve, a leading forecasting framework akin to a sommelier's guide for premium carbon markets. Early insights into the 2025 iteration of the Oxygen Conservation Curve, created in partnership with leading minds across the natural capital sector, suggested a robust upward trend, driven by tightening net-zero targets and escalating demand for verified high-integrity credits.

This trend gained momentum in 2024, when Nattergal achieved a record-breaking sale of credits at £84 tCO_2e, outperforming the Stockdale-Winter estimates of £51

tCO_2e. This sale underscored the market's growing appetite for quality and positioned high-grade credits like those in Oxygen Conservation's portfolio as premium assets poised for substantial appreciation.

For investors who wish to fund conservation projects and receive a return on the capital they have committed to environmental restoration, the Oxygen Conservation Carbon Curve provides the market-leading forward price projection for the premium carbon market. With its unparalleled quality and exclusivity, Oxygen Conservation's 2024 'vintage' sits firmly at the top of this curve.

Making the market for vintage carbon credits

The release of Oxygen Conservation's 2024 vintage was a market-making toast for the natural capital sector. By setting new standards for quality, transparency, and impact, the sale that we realised in 2025 underscored the growing value of premium carbon credits and reinforced the role of natural capital products as cornerstone assets in modern investment portfolios.

Since this piece was first drafted, we have been privileged to achieve a truly historic milestone: Oxygen Conservation has concluded a market-shaping transaction – a £1 million partnership for 8,000 premium UK credits priced at £125 per tonne. This landmark sale not only vindicates the vintage positioning of our 2024 credits, but also concretely demonstrates that high-integrity provenance-rich natural capital can command transformative prices and attract serious investment. The deal is a market-making event: it proves there is a deep, willing market for the very highest quality credits, and that the value of authenticity and stewardship is being recognised in cash terms.

Ross Fairley, senior partner of Burges Salmon, put the spirit of the deal succinctly:

> 'This partnership is about more than carbon – it's about setting a new standard for how we engage with nature and lead with purpose. We're proud to be working with Oxygen Conservation to build a model that others can learn from, replicate, and be inspired by.'

His firm's willingness to underwrite this premium price – to pay £125 per tonne to fund large-scale ecological restoration – is the clearest possible market validation of the vintage strategy.

This pivotal transaction reverberated across the sector, elevating the perceived value of other high-integrity natural capital products and services. It marked a turning point where sustainability-driven assets have become not only a moral imperative, but also a compelling financial opportunity.

For buyers and investors seeking to lead in this transformation, vintage natural capital products represent a defining chance to be part of the future of regenerative wealth creation.

On reflection

If behavioural economist and marketing icon Rory Sutherland were to stroll through the maturing vines of the natural capital market, I hope he'd raise a beautiful champagne flute to the 'psychological alchemy' (Sutherland, 2021) of positioning carbon credits as a vintage asset class.

'A Unique Vintage' was written with this in mind – inviting investors to think differently, to feel differently about environmental impact. It moves carbon from the realm of offsetting (cold, transactional, obligatory) into something rare, desirable, and even status-signalling. As Sutherland might put it, with his wonderfully eccentric flair, this is not about logic – it's about *meaning*. The perceived value lies not just in the tonnes of CO2e sequestered, but in the story behind it: the provenance, the exclusivity, the care. The terroir, which perhaps perfectly means the 'complete natural environment' (in which a particular wine is produced).

Sutherland often argues that 'a change in perspective is worth 80 IQ points'. That's exactly what this strategy offers. Rather than reducing carbon to a commodified burden, it reframes it as a premium investable product – something to collect, celebrate, and be proud of. Scarcity is a feature, not a flaw. Trust, traceability, and narrative become as important as the underlying carbon data.

Since the piece was first published, the market has only accelerated in this direction. Nattergal's landmark £1 million carbon sale to Arup – a deal valuing credits at £100 per tCO_2e – did more than break records. It sent a clear signal: buyers are no longer hunting for the cheapest offset. They're investing in provenance, in credibility, in confidence, and they're willing to pay for it.

The World's Only Genuine Natural Capital Portfolio

Written December 2024

Imagine an investment opportunity that delivers robust financial returns while yielding significant ecological dividends, all secured by tangible assets with inherent value. Welcome to Oxygen Conservation's natural capital portfolio – a high-impact diversified investment strategy that harmonises financial sustainability with environmental stewardship.

At the heart of our groundbreaking portfolio lies the land itself – a tangible asset offering unmatched downside protection. Spanning the terrains of England, Wales, and Scotland, our land holdings provide geographical diversification that mitigates risks while amplifying opportunities in conservation, renewable energy, and sustainable community development. This diversified physical asset base ensures that investments retain their intrinsic value regardless of market volatility and provide a hedge against inflation.

Premium carbon credits

Central to our portfolio are our premium carbon credits – the blue-chip stocks of the natural world. Verified under the UK Woodland Carbon Code and Peatland Code, these credits are more than abstract environmental offsets; they are grounded in the physical landscapes we own and manage, with each credit tied to a specific area of woodland or peatland that buyers can visit to see their carbon offsets for themselves.

By investing in woodlands and peatlands, we ensure that the value of our projects is secured not only by carbon sequestration, but also by the intrinsic worth of the land itself. This dual-asset approach provides a robust safety net, safeguarding investor value through well-managed estates that are both ecologically rich and economically sound.

Our transformative rewilding and biodiversity projects are the growth stocks in our portfolio – high-potential investments poised for significant long-term returns. By restoring natural processes, creating wildlife corridors, and reintroducing native species, we're regenerating ecosystems and enhancing the fundamental value of the land. Whether it's the majestic Scottish Highlands, the rolling hills of Wales, or England's lost wood pastures, these landscapes offer substantial residual value, ensuring resilience against market challenges while contributing to a richer, more diverse natural world.

Our renewable energy initiatives represent the dynamic growth potential of sustainable technology – comparable to high-performing tech equities. Wind power projects are not just forward-thinking investments; they are firmly rooted in the enduring stability of the land beneath them.

The assets strengthening our portfolio

Community engagement serves as the cornerstone of our sustainable development strategy, acting as the bond equivalent in our portfolio. Our extensive property holdings – including over forty homes and 100 agricultural buildings, along with early allocations or planning permissions for more than thirty additional properties – providing tangible lasting value, both financially and socially. These assets form the foundation of our community initiatives, generating stable returns and diversifying investment risk as well as supporting rural communities and directly addressing the housing crisis. Spread across England, Wales, and Scotland, they capture the inherent value of regional economic and social development.

Our unique ecotourism projects – from glamping sites to holiday cottages and wilderness escapes – are the high-value real estate investment trust (REIT) equivalents within our portfolio. Built on strategically located land that retains inherent value, these ventures offer both lifestyle investments and hedges against market shifts. They are more than profitable enterprises; they invite the public into the heart of our conservation mission, creating a symbiotic relationship between profitability and ecological awareness.

A diversified portfolio with balanced risk mitigation

Each asset in our portfolio is thoughtfully integrated to contribute to a harmonious balance of natural capital projects, renewable energy opportunities, and property-based returns. This diversified approach ensures that while some assets drive growth, others provide stability, creating a resilient investment landscape. Our geographical diversification across England, Wales, and Scotland further mitigates risk and captures regional policy benefits.

Investing in the future with tangible value

Oxygen Conservation isn't just investing in land; we're investing in the future. Our land assets offer a tangible safety net, maintaining value independently of market fluctuations. By aligning financial prosperity with environmental stewardship, we provide our investors with an opportunity to achieve strong returns without sacrificing social responsibility.

Investors no longer have to choose between profitability and purpose. Oxygen Conservation's natural capital portfolio delivers both, offering substantial financial returns and significant ecological benefits – all not just grounded in solid earth, but also cultivating a sustainable future for generations to come.

On reflection

I loved how this piece landed when it was first released. It marked a deliberate step in reframing our work – taking it from the environmental echo chamber and placing it squarely within the language of finance. As I've read more, listened more, and learned from some seriously wise counsel, my thinking has (and, of course, should) continued to evolve.

Here's where I've got to.

The rise in premium carbon credit prices – that's our **beta**. That's the market. The macro momentum behind high-integrity natural capital products. Confidence is building, and we're proud to be helping set the bar for what quality looks like. Carbon credits, when done right, can be the rising tide that lifts all boats – though there's probably a darker metaphor there about just how many boats we'll need if we fail to get this right.

Our **alpha** – our edge – isn't in the market. It's in the platform we've built. It's in our approach to land identification – and the boldness with which we act. It's in the speed of our decision making, the ambition we bring to every acquisition, and the operational model that turns vision into delivery. It's in the portfolio we've assembled, yes – but even more so, it's in the team we've brought together to deliver it. I genuinely believe we have the most disgracefully talented group working in this space anywhere in the world, and they're only getting better.

That's the bit you can't replicate. That's the competitive advantage you can't quantify. It's that talent – and the culture we've collectively built around it – that's enabled us to move from concept to execution faster than most thought possible. To make this portfolio real. To make it profitable. Most importantly, to make it matter.

Because in the end, it's not just about what we're investing in. It's about who's doing the investing – and why.

That's the alpha. That's Oxygen.

FIVE

Performance In The Wild

CULTure Shock: Why Scaling Should Feel Like Getting Better

Written July 2025

I was sitting with Oxygen Conservation's leadership team at a recent board meeting, discussing the careful balance between scaling the business to meet the increasing challenges and opportunities of our work, and the collective love we all feel for the special culture we've cultivated.

In his typically insightful way, our wonderfully wise head of people, Andrew, looked up and asked, 'Why do we always assume scaling a business will make the culture worse?'

Silence followed – not the awkward kind, but the rare kind that signals a collective realisation. Andrew, once again, had named a quiet truth hiding in plain sight. Why indeed would we assume that scaling must erode culture? In every other part of the business, we strive to attack challenges head-on, to improve relentlessly. We don't settle. We don't play safe, so why consider protection over enhancement when it comes to our culture? Why default to defence when our entire ethos is rooted in boldness?

This moment sparked a deeper reflection, and the answer became clear: our story is not one of cultural compromise, but of cultural ambition. It is the story of why and how we believe scaling should enhance, not erode, organisational culture – because that's exactly what we've done at Oxygen Conservation.

The culture advantage: Scaling boldly without losing your soul

The common business narrative goes like this: as companies scale, culture suffers. Growth becomes the villain. Expansion dilutes values. Process replaces passion.

What if this wasn't inevitable? What if scaling wasn't the enemy of culture, but an opportunity to make it even better? What if growth could actually serve as an accelerator for culture, intensifying, shaping, and strengthening it with each new phase of development?

At Oxygen Conservation, we've chosen a path that sees culture not as a relic to protect, but a force to project. If we don't settle for mediocrity in our environmental and social ambition, why would we accept cultural stagnation as the cost of progress? We're building something deliberately different – a conservation company delivering positive impact faster than tradition thinks possible, and a culture growing even stronger in the process.

The myth of cultural deterioration in scaling

Many leaders treat culture like glass – delicate, breakable, easily lost in the turbulence of (often too) rapid hiring and change. This fear-driven thinking creates the very conditions it dreads: rushed recruitment, diminished standards, and a culture of compromise. The deeper issue is the belief that culture is inherently fragile, when in truth, it is one of the most evolutionarily resilient and adaptive forces in a company's DNA – capable of maturing, morphing, and strengthening in step with the business it serves.

The fear of cultural change is not just operational; it's psychological. Scarcity mindsets fuel defensive strategies. Leaders worry about losing what made them special, so they cling to the present instead of designing the future. Diversity of thought becomes a risk rather than a resource. The moment you fear cultural change, you start hiring for sameness, and sameness stifles innovation. You build echo chambers instead of ecosystems of ideas. If you seek to protect as opposed to enhance, you're already moving backwards.

Culture, like any living system, isn't preserved by stasis. It's elevated by evolution. Scaling isn't a cultural hazard; it's a cultural opportunity, but only if you're bold enough to embrace change with purpose.

Oxygen Conservation's experience: A contrarian perspective

From day one at Oxygen Conservation, we've had cultural ambition. Not just to do good work, but to build a team that *feels* different. We wanted to prove that professionalism and personality could coexist, and that a mission-driven culture could be magnetically compelling.

We've always said we don't want lots of people – we want lots of *impact*. Our ambition isn't headcount; it's positive environmental, social, and economic impact. Each person we bring in must raise the bar, not just meet the standard. Our hiring is less about filling gaps and more about expanding potential. We ask: how will this person make us better?

We're building a team of adventurous, environmentally obsessed, mission-driven rebels who challenge each other and elevate the whole. Every addition must make us better in a *meaningful* way. Every hire is a cultural multiplier, never just a box ticked.

When we first opened roles, we were stunned by the hundreds of applications. Now? Thousands, and not just any applicants – top-tier minds from elite institutions, unconventional paths, and passionate corners of the conservation world. The brand we've built around mission and authenticity has attracted people who want more than a job – they want purpose.

We often ask ourselves, 'Would our earliest team members get hired today?' not as a criticism, but as a celebration of how far we've come. We're not about loyalty to the past; we're about commitment to the future. Every year, we must raise the bar – better systems, sharper processes, stronger brand, broader reach. We must constantly reassess what excellent looks like.

Here's the truth: every good business is a recruitment business. It's a founder's job to lead that charge. Culture is shaped at the point of entry, and talent is your most scalable lever for impact.

Hiring for the future, not the present

Too many organisations hire for today. We don't. We hire for tomorrow. For the version of Oxygen Conservation that doesn't exist yet, but should. Candidates need to fit the aspirational culture – not just the current one.

That means we're not looking for people who fit in. We want people who stretch us – who challenge our assumptions, bring new dimensions, and leave us better. We call it CULTure for a reason: it's intentional, intense, and unlike anything else. It's not always comfortable, but growth rarely is.

The team at Oxygen Conservation is deeply involved in hiring because culture isn't a top-down edict – it's a shared experience. Candidates meet the team. They hear the good, the bad, the bonkers. They know what they're signing up for. We believe in radical transparency from day one – that way, expectations are aligned, and commitment is genuine.

Lessons from elite sport: Continuous offensive strategy

In elite sport, top teams don't coast. They stay on the offensive. They recruit like they're behind. They train like they've never won, because complacency is kryptonite. Championship winning teams invest relentlessly in culture, because they know it's the foundation for sustained success.

We apply the same logic to culture. Our goal isn't to protect what we've built – it's to push it. To ask every week: how do we make this better, more transparent, more energised, more aligned to our unreasonable ambition? Our culture isn't a comfort zone; it's a performance zone.

The moment you play cultural defence, you've already lost. The game is always changing – and the best teams evolve with it.

Culture is dynamic, not static

Culture isn't a mural on the wall. It's a movement in the hall. It breathes. It flexes. It changes – and it should. Companies that cling to cultural nostalgia often find themselves outpaced by those who embrace cultural momentum.

We don't fear change. We *architect* it. Through regular check-ins, cultural audits, and open feedback loops, we make sure the culture evolves with us. Remote working isn't a barrier – it's an opportunity to craft a closeness rooted in purpose, not proximity. We've built digital rituals that create intimacy, accountability, and alignment.

At Oxygen Conservation, we don't have a 'vibe'. We have a mission, and that's more powerful than any ping-pong table or beanbag ever could be. We measure culture by connection, not convenience.

Practical strategies for cultural scaling

How do you scale culture without diluting it? Here's what works for us:

- Compete for talent like your mission depends on it, because it does.
- Recruit slowly and deliberately. Never compromise.
- Make CULTure part of the pitch. It's your competitive advantage.
- Be radically transparent. People can't live the values if they don't see them in action.
- Fire with kindness, but also with clarity. Culture isn't just who you hire – it's who you let go.
- Celebrate the cultural wins. Recognise the behaviours that build the future.
- Stay humble. Stay hungry. Stay learning. Culture dies when curiosity does.

The results are clear: our team is cohesive, our mission defined, and our work effective. We are executing projects quickly and efficiently, expanding the delivery of natural capital products, and enhancing our brand recognition through consistent values and performance.

Internally, alignment has improved across the organisation, and externally, we are recognised for both the quality and integrity of our work. These improvements are not accidental – they reflect deliberate efforts to maintain and enhance our culture as we grow.

We assess our cultural success through everyday behaviours: how we handle challenges, celebrate achievements, and support one another when no one is watching. These are the signs that our culture is not only intact, but thriving.

Future-proofing your culture

There is no 'final form' of your culture. The goal isn't to arrive. It's to *adapt* – perpetually. Culture is not an endpoint; it's evolution.

That's why at Oxygen Conservation, we embed a growth mindset at every level. We train. We stretch. We fail forward. We celebrate progress, not perfection. We treat cultural evolution as an essential business function. Culture is not an HR task. It's a leadership obsession, and it must be measured not just in sentiment, but in strategic advantage.

Scaling doesn't have to kill culture. In fact, it can improve it – if you do it on purpose. Growth is the great revealer. It shows you who you are, what you value, and whether your culture is real or rhetoric.

At Oxygen Conservation, we've found that growth isn't a threat to our culture. It's the amplifier of impact.

Here's the challenge. Don't settle. Don't play defence. Don't mourn the culture you had. Build the culture you *need*. Relentlessly. Boldly. Unreasonably.

Because the best culture is not the one you protect.

It's the one you're creating!

On reflection

I have little to add to the article above, but I would like to take the opportunity to recognise something and someone incredibly important. Our culture at Oxygen Conservation did not appear by accident. It wasn't conjured out of thin air during a branding session or written neatly onto a slide. It was built, carefully, deliberately, obsessively, over more than fifteen years of collaboration with someone who has shaped my thinking more profoundly than almost anyone else: Dr Andrew Dewar.

Andrew has been my closest thought partner on people, performance, psychology, and CULTure for longer than Oxygen Conservation has existed. We have worked through every detail together. Not just the big ideas, but the small ones too. The subtle ones. The ones most leaders never even notice, let alone spend time debating. If there is a sentence, a structure, or a system in our people strategy that feels intuitive or elegant or quietly powerful, the odds are that Andrew played a key role in shaping it.

Across more than fifteen years of friendship, many of those working together, we have built a culture that means the world to us. That feels alive because Andrew treats culture as something living. That feels precise because he refuses to let anything be vague. That feels human because he never forgets that behind every KPI sits an actual person with fears, ambition, brilliance, and flaws.

I often get credited publicly for the culture at Oxygen Conservation, but the truth is simple. Without Andrew, the culture we have today would not exist. Not even come close.

He is the person who asks the piercing questions at exactly the right moment, who spots the psychological nuance others miss, who finds clarity where the rest of us see confusion. He is the reason we never slip into lazy thinking about people or performance. He is the quiet force ensuring we remain bold but grounded, ambitious but aligned, intense but supportive.

Fifteen years of partnership is rare in business. Fifteen years of shared obsession, shared ambition, and shared belief in what great culture can do is rarer still. Oxygen Conservation would not be the place it is without Andrew. I would not be the leader I am without him, and the journey we are on together remains one of the most meaningful and enjoyable collaborations of my life.

How to Stop Having Terrible Team Meetings: What We've Learned from Blackstone Mondays

Written June 2025

Let's be honest – most team meetings are a colossal waste of time. They're boring, predictable, and joyless – barely scratching the surface of what actually matters. You join, you nod, you check your inbox on the side – and leave wondering what just happened.

It doesn't have to be that way.

What are Blackstone Mondays?

At Oxygen Conservation, we've built a meeting format that fuels clarity, fires up momentum, and connects our team at a whole new level. We call it *Blackstone Mondays*, and no exaggeration, it's a game-changer. It's the most valuable hour of our week, and it might just be the most important ritual in our entire company.

Here are the essential components of a Blackstone Monday:

Begin with purpose

If you don't start with a reason to be in the room (even if that room's virtual), you're already behind. Every Blackstone Monday kicks off with a crystal-clear objective to inspire, align, and connect. It's a set piece, not a slot filler. These are strategic briefings, not glorified status updates.

We share intel across climate finance, rewilding strategy, operational progress, and leadership lessons. Everyone leaves feeling sharper, faster, and more focused on what matters that week. The goal isn't just to update – it's to equip and energise.

Embrace remote collaboration, intentionally

We're proudly a remote-first business. That's not a workaround – it's a weapon. Our team spans geographies, terrains, and sometimes time zones, yet Monday meetings bring us together.

Blackstone is our heartbeat, our operating system. We don't confuse being present with being effective. It's not about logging on – it's about showing up. We bring our full attention, full selves, and full ambition to the virtual room. When everyone's switched on, magic happens.

Design a flexible, purposeful structure

Static agendas are where good ideas go to die, and they're boring. That's why we keep our structure solid, but flexible. Core components – weekly wins, strategic challenges, rapid-fire updates – create consistency, but we leave space for what's real and relevant. It's about creating room for truth, for boldness, for breakthrough thinking. Some of our best decisions and biggest shifts started as impromptu questions mid-call. That's creative chaos. That's culture.

Democratise the conversation

Great ideas don't care about job titles. That's why at Oxygen Conservation, everyone speaks. From brand-new interns to the leadership team, the mic is open. No permission needed.

Blackstone Mondays flatten hierarchy and amplify insight. We believe in the power of fresh perspective. Your second week on the job might just be the moment you ask the question that changes everything. That's how we win.

Explain the why

We don't just talk about what needs to get done – we talk about *why* it matters. These meetings are where our values show up in real time. We dig into challenges, own mistakes, share progress, and ask big questions. What are we learning about land ownership? How do we engage better with local communities? What happens when nature, finance, and politics collide? Blackstone is where we wrestle with complexity and connect our day-to-day work to our long-term vision.

Recognition and celebration

We don't save praise for performance reviews. Recognition is part of the rhythm. Each week, we call out wins – big and small. A project breakthrough. A well-handled conflict. A moment of outstanding leadership. Yes, sometimes just being a great teammate.

Recognition doesn't cost a thing, but it builds culture, accelerates engagement, and reminds everyone that their work matters. We're unashamedly loud and vocal about this. Our meetings are celebratory and include a lot of clapping.

Learning and continuous improvement

Every Blackstone Monday is a feedback loop. What worked? What didn't? What needs adjusting? We treat the meeting itself as a product – always refining, always improving. We coach a lot. We share articles, tools, frameworks. We unpack recent decisions. We dig into what success looks like, not just where we're falling short. This isn't feedback theatre. This is about real-time iteration, and the pace is fast.

Be radically transparent

Transparency isn't a buzzword – it's a muscle, and we work it hard. We share what's going well *and* what's not. We talk openly about numbers, narratives, and near-misses. We say the hard stuff out loud, not because it's uncomfortable, but because it's necessary. Radical transparency builds trust, creates accountability, and saves weeks of passive-aggressive back-channelling. We choose candour over comfort.

Debate and discuss

High-performing teams don't dodge tension, they move through it. That's why we use our Blackstone Mondays to surface the difficult conversations. Disagreement isn't dysfunction – it's design. We debate decisions, tackle ethical dilemmas, and question assumptions.

When people feel safe to challenge, you get sharper thinking and stronger alignment. Some of our most courageous choices were forged in the friendly fire of a good-faith full-squad disagreement, and we're better for it.

Access to decision makers

You can't build trust in the dark, so we turn on the lights. The leadership team is not just in the room – we're in the conversation. We're visible, responsive, and accountable. Questions are asked and answered. Decisions are explained, not announced. It's not about being perfect – it's about being present, human, and willing to own it when we get something wrong. That kind of leadership invites people in. It builds belief.

Blackstone Mondays are more than meetings – they're our launch pad. It's the biggest privilege as a leader to start every week by listening to and coaching our entire business. It's where we recalibrate our compass for the week ahead. We check alignment, focus energy, and reset priorities. It's the pulse check that ensures we're moving fast in the right direction, not just running hard in circles.

Every organisation has rituals. This is ours. It's our chance to reconnect with the mission, recommit to the team, and raise the standard again.

On reflection

If your meetings drain energy instead of generating it – burn them down and rebuild. Start with purpose. Build for performance. Make every meeting real, make it useful, and make it yours.

For us, Blackstone Monday is a weekly rhythm of alignment, ambition, and action. For you? This could be the start of a meeting culture that people love and that actually delivers positive impact and performance.

Recruiting for the Unknown: Lessons from Bletchley Park for Scaling Conservation

Written December 2025

Every generation has its crucible – a situation of severe trial. In the 1940s, it was the Second World War. For us today, it is the intertwined crises of climate change and biodiversity collapse.

At Bletchley Park, the challenge was breaking codes to safeguard lives and secure victory. At Oxygen Conservation, the challenge is breaking the entrenched codes of conservation, land ownership, economics, and investment to secure a liveable future. Both required, and still require, something radical in recruitment. Not hiring for known tasks, but for the unknown. Not for jobs neatly defined, but for problems not yet written down. At Bletchley, this meant recruiting linguists, mathematicians, classicists, and crossword champions – people with aptitude. Today, in building the natural capital economy, it means something strikingly similar!

The genius of Bletchley Park was that it recruited for potential. It valued aptitude over adherence and creativity over conformity. The same lesson applies now in our mission to Scale Conservation. We must recruit and nurture people who can solve problems we haven't yet imagined, in a world changing faster than ever before.

Talent over titles

At the outbreak of the war, Commander Alastair Denniston and later operational head Edward Travis knew that Bletchley Park could not rely on the rigid hierarchies of the military or civil service. The codebreaking huts needed fresh thinking, rapid experimentation, and people who could rewire their brains in real-time. They hired expert chess players, men – and women – with a gift for pattern recognition, and young people who could see beyond the obvious.

This spirit is alive in Oxygen Conservation's recruitment. Our people strategy is intentional and direct: we hire for the ceiling, not the floor. We're not looking for people who fit today's job description; we're looking for people who will outgrow it, who will make us better in ways we cannot yet predict. Just as the huts at Bletchley Park were full of brilliant misfits, we deliberately seek those who challenge us, who bring new perspectives from sport, finance, technology, media, agriculture, and art.

Conservation is no longer just about counting birds or planting trees – and it certainly isn't about writing yet another report detailing how much worse things have become. It's about innovation, thermal drone surveying, artificial intelligence, geographical information systems, financial models, land acquisitions, carbon pricing curves, biodiversity metrics, storytelling, and sensitive stakeholder negotiations. The game has changed, and so have the players.

Meritocracy of minds

Denniston encouraged and Travis preserved a culture that was unlike the rigid commands of the services. A culture where hierarchy, though not absent, was relaxed. What mattered was not rank, but results. In Hut 8 – Alan Turing's famous hub – if you had the idea that broke the Enigma, it didn't matter whether you were a twenty-year-old Cambridge undergraduate or a senior battle-hardened naval officer.

That's the atmosphere we cultivate and where we thrive. At Oxygen Conservation, challenge is not just tolerated; it's expected. Harmony, we argue, is overrated. Our greatest achievements are built on what we call respectful disagreement. In practice, this means questioning bad ideas, improving them through debate, and holding strong opinions loosely. The goal is not consensus; the goal is progress.

Like Bletchley, where innovation was born from intellectual sparring, our culture thrives on friction. In conservation, comfortable consensus leads to small, safe projects and little to no progresses. Respectful disagreement builds movement and momentum!

Rebel rulebook

Bletchley Park mathematician Gordon Welchman in his book *The Hut Six Story: Breaking the Enigma Codes* (1997) reflected on the lessons of Bletchley and suggested something radical: people with rare skills should not have to climb a managerial ladder to achieve prestige or pay. In fact, he argued, a brilliant mathematician should be able to earn more than the director, without ever being forced into a managerial role.

At Oxygen Conservation, we've borrowed heavily from this. Our system doesn't just reward management. It rewards impact, ideas, and execution. We separate performance into tiers – elite, high, and elsewhere – not by title, but by output. We're unashamed in saying that if you're world-class in your field, you should be rewarded for it, whether or not you manage a single person.

Though counter-cultural in most organisations, in Oxygen Conservation, this is necessary. Forcing brilliant conservationists into management kills their brilliance and starves the system of innovation. We'd rather they stay brilliant, pushing the frontiers of natural capital, carbon pricing, or ecological restoration – and be rewarded accordingly.

Diversity as a weapon

Another lesson from Bletchley is the sheer power of diversity. By recruiting women in large numbers – still revolutionary in the 1940s – and by drawing from classics, history, engineering, and languages, Bletchley created an unparalleled cognitive concoction. The result was not just more ideas, but better ones.

We take the same view. Excluding groups of people – by accident or by design – shrinks the talent pool. Worse, it shrinks the imagination of the organisation. Our conviction is that cognitive diversity matters more than technical similarity. A mathematician and an ecologist (or a former pilot and a former model) will approach a land management problem differently, and the collision of those perspectives is where progress lies. Fortunately, at Oxygen Conservation we have all four.

Cognitive diversity doesn't just come from biology. It comes from upbringing, culture, failures, experiences, and adventure. That's why we deliberately recruit from outside the environment sector. We're building a team that thinks differently, because conservation at scale is a puzzle too complex for one discipline to solve.

Cryptography and conservation

Cryptography is a paradoxical science. Its value is maximised by secrecy, yet its rigour depends on professional exchange. The Bletchley codebreakers worked in closed communities, publishing their research and learnings only decades later.

Conservation shares this paradox. Transparency is vital for investor trust, for community support, for market credibility, but this is not always the case. Some of our work at Oxygen Conservation requires strategic opacity. We don't share every acquisition in the moment; we protect sensitive negotiations. This balance, between openness and secrecy, is one we walk carefully, just as the people at Bletchley did.

There is another link: both cryptography and conservation are fields where speed matters. A code broken too late is useless. A peatland restored too late might be equally useless. At Bletchley, signals travelled to London at increased scale and speed. Today, the natural capital economy in the time of AI needs an even greater increase in scale and speed.

Building a talent pipeline

If Bletchley Park was the talent factory of the 1940s, we want Oxygen Conservation to be the academy of the 2020s. Our intern programme is explicitly designed as an academy system. We don't just hire for today; we train for tomorrow. We rotate people across estates, projects, and disciplines. We expose them to finance, ecology, and operations. We set the bar high – deliberately so.

This is not elitism. It's urgency. Conservation can no longer be the domain of volunteers and retirees. We need business athletes – people capable of operating at investment pace, capable of working across disciplines, and capable of delivering scale. Just as Bletchley recruited crossword champions and chess players, we recruit athletes, creatives, engineers, and adventurers – because excellence in one domain often signals the mindset we need in another.

Respectful disagreement as culture

We've coined a phrase that mirrors the challenge culture of Bletchley: respectfully disagree. Harmony feels nice, but it rarely moves the needle. The work of conservation is too urgent, too complex to be left to groupthink.

Our culture insists on questioning. We expect everyone – interns included – to challenge decisions, to ask awkward questions, to find flaws. It's not always comfortable, but it is always productive. When someone says, 'I respectfully disagree', we lean in, because the alternative – comfortable silence – is the death of progress.

Lessons for Scaling Conservation

Recruiting for jobs not yet created to solve problems not yet defined was Bletchley Park's genius. It must be ours too. The people we are bringing in today will be solving crises tomorrow that we cannot yet see.

As Welchman argued, brilliance must be rewarded on its own terms. As Denniston proved, hierarchy must bend to innovation. As Bletchley's culture of cognitive diversity showed, the best ideas often come from the most unexpected places.

Scaling Conservation is not just a technical challenge. It is a human one. The code to be broken is not just ecological, but organisational. If Oxygen Conservation can recruit, nurture, and unleash the next generation of misfits, rebels, and innovators, then just as Bletchley Park rewrote history, perhaps we can too.

On reflection

This article draws inspiration from the book *Counter-Intelligence* by Robert Hannigan (2024) and the extraordinary history it documents. My thanks go to Bletchley Park itself – and to Alan Turing and his fellow codebreakers – for the enduring lessons they left us in innovation, diversity, and courage under pressure.

Finally, a personal note of gratitude to my wife, Helen, who first introduced me to the story of Bletchley Park during her dissertation. Without that spark, these reflections, and perhaps our entire approach to people and culture at Oxygen Conservation, would be very different. Then again, without Helen, so would I!

Masters and Apprentices: Mentorship that Flows Both Ways

Written August 2025

At Oxygen Conservation, we believe in Scaling Conservation and careers. We have so many powerful tools for doing both, including tech, finance, and natural capital, but one of the most powerful is mentorship. It's the exchange of wisdom for energy, of experience for enthusiasm, and it has the potential to change not only individuals, but entire organisations.

We call mentorship the Master and Apprentice Model, and when it's done right, it's alchemy. It's a system as old as craft itself, but more relevant now than ever in a world moving faster than most can comprehend. We're building a new asset class in real time, and this model is our cultural infrastructure – our academy, our succession plan, our talent pipeline, our edge. It allows us to develop from within, scaling not only what we know, but how we do it.

What the master gives

The master doesn't just teach – they shape. They explain, demonstrate, challenge, and protect. They open doors and design experiences that they themselves may no longer appreciate. What is mundane to them – making a call, organising an estate visit, researching a report – becomes magical to the apprentice. The everyday becomes extraordinary when seen through fresh eyes, and that is the point. The apprentice reminds the master of the value of what they know and appreciates the value of what is being shared and given.

The master sets the standards. They embody what excellence looks like, but crucially, they pass it on. With time, they even help their apprentice surpass them. That's the plan. That's the point. Legacy isn't about clinging to power – it's about multiplying it. Sportspeople talk about the coaching tree, with branches of mentorship spreading off from the trunk (the initial coach), and we want Oxygen Conservation to be a similar incubator of future incredible startup businesses.

When the master invests fully, they benefit too. They gain perspective, sharpen their own thinking, and are reminded of why they do what they do. They also gain more of their time back to focus on new projects, fresh experiences, and the things they want to learn. The relationship becomes mutual enrichment.

What the apprentice gives

The apprentice, in return, must earn their place. They take on the weight. They carry the bags, do the boring stuff, the repetitive stuff, the thankless tasks – organise the meetings, write up minutes and actions, summarise documents, and even sometimes find cool coffee shops on road trips. It's the cost of tuition. It's where humility meets hunger. It's how they earn their education – we've all done it, and in many ways, we continue to do so every day.

The apprentice must be willing to fail, and more importantly, willing to learn from it. They must ask the apparently stupid questions (it's rare any question is actually stupid), do the tasks that no one sees, and keep showing up even when the work is hard, boring, and repetitive.

However, they don't do this alone. Failure is never final. It's caught, coached, corrected. In public, the apprentice is praised. In private, they are challenged. Always protected, but never coddled.

This is a system built on radical candour – caring personally while challenging directly (Scott, 2017). We at Oxygen Conservation have seen this work spectacularly – across estates, in the investment teams, through carbon deals to the podcast studio. This isn't the forced, inauthentic corporate mentorship rhetoric – it's the real thing, happening every day. Real life. Real responsibility. Real growth.

Reverse mentoring: The hidden power

The magic of this model doesn't just flow one way. Some of our most exciting developments – whether it's applying AI automation to our people processes, streamlining workflows, or redefining our entire recruitment process – have come from apprentices showing the way forward.

The next generation doesn't just want a seat at the table. They bring the table, the chairs, and the tech to run the meeting. They teach us new ways of thinking, working, learning. In doing so, they challenge the master to grow too.

This is reverse mentorship in action. A dynamic loop of growth. A two-way street paved with curiosity and collaboration, because in the best cases, the apprentice doesn't just learn – they teach. They innovate. They transform the model.

For example, what began as a classic mentoring relationship at Oxygen Conservation quickly became more: a creative and operational partnership. The apprentice, Archie Barnes, brought digital transformation, a completely new outlook (email pun intended) on life, and an unreasonableness in his drive to provide a unique experience. The master, Charles Owen, brought decades of experience, exacting standards, and an absolute refusal to compromise on quality and delivery. Together, they allowed each other to succeed, and as a result, Charles was able to step fully away from the Estate he'd lived and loved for almost fifteen years, appointing Archie as his successor. As Estate manager, Archie now has his own wonderful apprentice.

We've seen apprentices shape the way we manage estates, build content, rethink finance models, and even influence the tone of voice we use as a business. These aren't side projects – they're pivotal contributions that push us forward. When this mutual exchange happens with openness and trust, the entire business shifts. New efficiencies emerge. Bold ideas surface. Momentum builds.

What happens when the apprentice outgrows the role?

The role changes. The business expands. We back them.

Sometimes they take on their own apprentice. Sometimes they spin out into new roles or – hopefully in the future – their own companies. When they do, we support them – with guidance, with connections, even with capital. Why would we spend years helping someone become exceptional and then not want to be part of their future? It's not losing – it's winning.

At Oxygen Conservation, we're professionalising conservation. That means every team member is also a leader, every good leader is a teacher, and every hire is a platform-building decision.

The primary job of a founder or CEO is talent identification, attraction, and development. If you're not doing it, your business is failing. If you're not recruiting people better than you, then the business is getting worse. That's why we set such a high bar.

When we Scale Conservation, we also have to scale character, skill, ambition, and care. We have to create systems that grow people as well as profits. If we do that well, then we all become masters, and we all remain apprentices.

On reflection

If there's one lesson our Master and Apprentice Model has taught us more clearly than anything else, it's this: the business world has wildly overvalued experience and consistently undervalued talent. We see it everywhere. CVs padded with years, not outcomes. Job specs written like museum plaques, venerating longevity instead of capability. Entire industries selecting for tenure rather than trajectory.

When we look at our own team – the people who have built the UK's largest natural capital portfolio at unprecedented speed – the pattern is unmistakable. Talent beats experience.

Hunger beats history. Curiosity beats comfort. Every. Single. Time.

This is our *Moneyball* realisation (Lewis, 2004). Just as Billy Beane, visionary general manager of Oakland Athletic, ignored the old myths of baseball and bet on undervalued attributes that actually predicted performance, we're doing the same in conservation and capital. We're betting on intelligence, adaptability, character, rate of learning, ambition, and audacity. We're betting on people who grow faster than the company, not people who have been around longer than the market.

The truth is simple. Experience can tell you what has been done – somewhere else for someone else. Talent shows you what is possible. Experience clings to the familiar. Talent builds the future. Experience maintains. Talent transforms.

The Master and Apprentice Model works so well at Oxygen Conservation because it rejects the outdated assumption that value increases automatically with age or time served. We don't hire for the past. We hire for potential. We don't promote because someone has waited long enough. We promote because someone has earned it, proved it, delivered it.

In a world moving as fast as ours, experience ages quickly. Talent compounds. That is why we've built a culture where the juniors can challenge the seniors, the inexperienced can outperform the seasoned, and the apprentices can rise to become masters. We see it happening already. It's not an accident. It's the strategy.

Scaling Conservation means scaling talent. Not protecting hierarchy. Not worshipping time served. Not mistaking seniority for superiority. It means finding brilliant people early, backing them hard, and giving them the runway to change the game and maybe even the world.

Gegenpressing the Bureaucracy: Playing the Fast Game in a Slow System

Written November 2025

In elite football, gegenpressing is more than a defensive tactic. It's an operating philosophy brought to life wonderfully by the mercurial Jürgen Klopp. When possession is lost, the team immediately applies intense pressure not to recover the ball eventually, but to recover it before the opponent has time to think. By compressing time and space, gegenpressing turns defence into attack. It flips hesitation into momentum.

At Oxygen Conservation, we've discovered that this philosophy doesn't just belong on the pitch – it's the way to win against bureaucracy. We've learned that bureaucracy is not a wall to crash into, but a system to outpace, overwhelm, and transform into momentum for positive change.

Bureaucracy thrives on delay. Requests for more detail. Another form. Another meeting. Another committee. Another draft. The system is designed to elongate the game, stretching it into extra time until momentum (and almost always enthusiasm) dies. In most industries, that's simply frustrating. In conservation, it's devastating.

Nature doesn't wait. Neither does climate change. Every delay is biodiversity lost, carbon released, opportunities missed. If we want to Scale Conservation at the speed demanded by ecological reality, we cannot afford to play bureaucracy on its terms. The longer we spend filling in forms, responding to repeated questions, or completing another report, the less time we spend restoring peatlands, planting woodland, or creating habitats where wildlife can thrive.

Delay is the silent killer of conservation and the death of financial returns.

The gegenpressing approach

Instead of waiting, at Oxygen Conservation, we press. Hard, fast, and smart. Gegenpressing bureaucracy is about turning every slowing mechanism into an accelerator, every pause into progress, every barrier into an opening.

Here's how we've applied gegenpressing principles to bureaucracy:

1. Urgency is strategy

When feedback lands on our desk, we turn it around in hours, not weeks. Bureaucracy expects drift; we respond with decisive acceleration. By denying delay, the oxygen bureaucracy feeds on, we maintain control of the tempo. Urgency isn't just about speed – it's about setting the tone. We show that we will not be the ones slowing things down, and in doing so, we force others to move with us.

Urgency also means refusing to accept no as the end of the story. If we don't get a yes, we don't stop. We research, collaborate, and work relentlessly with our partners until we do. If the answer is still no, we publish and share what we've learned so others don't waste time on the same dead ends. We call out bureaucracy when it blocks progress and push for sector-wide change. Urgency is persistence with teeth; it's the refusal to let delay dictate the outcome, for the sake of others and our future selves.

2. Pre-emptive precision

We never just answer the question asked. We answer the next five as well. By anticipating where scrutiny will go, we close down lines of resistance before they open.

Detailed, specific language leaves no room for bureaucratic ambiguity. Think of it as closing down passing lanes before the opponent even sees them. If you know where the questions are going, you can take the sting out before they're asked.

This isn't theory – it comes from experience. Public bodies only have so many cards they can play, and their moves are repetitive and predictable. That means we can prepare answers before we even apply. We know the big hitters and the greatest hits. We address each one in advance, removing excuses before they're raised. Precision isn't about wordplay; it's about foresight, preparation, and stripping bureaucracy of the time it feeds on.

3. Overdeliver by design

When we're asked for more information, we see it as an opportunity. More detail means more space to demonstrate clarity of thought, depth of evidence, and alignment with outcomes. What frustrates others, we weaponise. We give context, evidence, forecasts, and case studies, ensuring that by the time the reader reaches the end of our response, the only possible conclusion is yes. Bureaucracy cannot argue with overwhelming clarity.

4. Champions in the system

Because every gegenpress relies on players who can read the game, we build relationships inside the bureaucracy. We look for the champions who want projects to succeed and, crucially, who have the authority to make it happen. We align our outcomes with their policies, objectives, and occasionally passions.

Suddenly, the system starts working with us instead of against us. These champions become our midfield generals – dictating tempo, seeing space, and unlocking opportunities hidden in red tape. Because influence matters, we aim high – the captains of the team who can bring about real change within the bureaucracy. Transparency in these relationships matters too: we share openly, remove suspicion, and create momentum by showing we are here to move fast, together.

5. Momentum is contagious

We frame our submissions not as boxes ticked, but as accelerators. Instead of neutralising energy, we create it. Bureaucracy is built to slow things down. We make it easier to say yes than no.

When one approval moves quickly, others follow. Speed breeds confidence. Momentum builds a narrative: this project is different; this one is unstoppable.

Once one project is not only approved, but delivered flawlessly, the Oxygen Conservation name builds trust and integrity with public bodies. They know what to expect, they know we deliver, and confidence grows. That trust means the next project usually moves faster, because speed follows speed. Our reputation becomes its own press, carrying us into the next challenge with greater momentum.

6. Aligning with outcomes

We never forget that bureaucracy isn't arbitrary; it exists, at least in theory, to ensure outcomes, so we show how our outcomes deliver on its. Biodiversity recovery, carbon storage, flood resilience, community benefits – by aligning our goals with institutional priorities, we create a positive-sum game.

By working with us, public bodies achieve their own targets too – whether it's 30x30 (30% of the world's land and ocean areas to be protected by 2030), net zero, or climate resilience – and we do the heavy lifting to make it happen. Instead of asking for permission, we help them succeed. We become the easiest route to their own wins, the delivery unit for the most entrenched bureaucracies.

Professionalising pace

These principles are not reckless. They're professionalisation, or in the language of the financial sector, sophistication of process. Conservation is no longer a slow, soft pursuit. It's an investable asset class where internal rates of return (IRRs), carbon credits, and biodiversity units sit alongside ecological restoration and community impact.

Just as in elite sport, pace changes the skills required. To thrive, we must combine ecological expertise with financial literacy, operational excellence, and relentless tempo. Professionalisation is the foundation that makes gegenpressing possible.

In football, gegenpressing is exhausting. It demands fitness, discipline, and belief in the system. The same is true here. This approach is not the easy way – it requires rigour, resilience, and constant readiness. Every member of the team has to be tuned in, ready to close down space, ready to deliver at speed – another reason why we prioritise recruitment and talent attraction above almost everything else we do.

When the stakes are this high, there is no alternative. Conservation can no longer be played at walking pace.

Bureaucracy will never vanish, but we can refuse to play on its terms. We can press harder, move faster, and dictate the tempo, because while bureaucracy is designed to protect itself, we are here to protect something infinitely more important: the future of nature, people, prosperity, and planet.

In the end, gegenpressing the bureaucracy is not just about speed and effort – it's about survival. If we keep pressing, we don't just win the ball back. We win time, opportunity, and momentum for the living systems that cannot wait. We show that conservation can play at the highest level: fast, decisive, and impossible to ignore.

On reflection

No one exhibits this approach better than our wonderful head of environment and the very first member of Oxygen Conservation, Dan Johnson. I therefore asked Dan to reflect on this article with a real-world example.

One of the clearest illustrations of this approach was our experience securing a Flood Risk Activity Permit for a transformational project within the portfolio. Despite the comprehensive application we submitted with mitigation standards well above the industry norm (whatever that means), the process still took more than six months to conclude. At times, it felt like a test of stamina more than substance. When we pressed for an update, the regulator's response was to send five more questions – one of which was whether the project had any public health, environmental, or economic impacts. Our answer, of course, was an emphatic yes, setting out how the project would restore a failing waterbody, reduce local flood risk, create species-rich habitats, and generate economic value by directly engaging local contractors. It was the sort of question that revealed less about our project and more about the system we were navigating.

This is where experience and diplomacy matter. It would be easy to grow cynical when faced with questions that appear designed to delay rather than decide. Instead, we treat them as openings. Each request is a chance to reinforce the project's value, to make it harder for bureaucrats to say no, and to underline the alignment between our objectives and theirs. In this way, even a stalling tactic becomes another platform to demonstrate leadership, competence, and the ecological urgency of our work.

Of course, even the best-prepared applications sometimes need more than technical excellence; they need champions. Letters of support from senior leaders and trusted collaborators become invaluable here. They provide not just evidence, but credibility. They show regulators that this is not one organisation pushing an agenda, but a coalition of respected voices backing a shared vision. In footballing terms, they are our midfield generals, spotting the killer pass and opening up the play when the space seems impossibly tight.

While bureaucracy will always favour caution, our lesson is to turn that weight against itself. By responding fast, answering fully, and enlisting allies who share our goals, we move the game forward on our terms. If there's a touch of irony in needing to justify environmental benefits in an environmental permitting process, we can at least say we did so with clarity, confidence, and a measure of humour. We turned a six-month delay into six more reasons why the project must go ahead.

Why Unpaid Internships are Failing the Environment Sector – and How We Can Fix It

Written October 2024

The environment sector has asked people to work for free for too long. It's one of the reasons it hasn't been considered investable – it wouldn't even invest in itself!

Unpaid work – whether disguised as internships, volunteer roles, or valuable experience – is an outdated practice that undermines progress by limiting diversity and excluding new talent. It's time to throw out the 'way we've always done things' and reimagine internships as genuine investments in both people and the planet.

Investing in talent, diversity, and passion

I recently responded to a LinkedIn question by confirming that 'all our internships are paid, otherwise they're not internships, they're work experience'. Unpaid internships create enormous barriers to entry, particularly for those from disadvantaged backgrounds. How can we expect the brightest, most creative minds to lead the fight against biodiversity collapse and climate change if we refuse to pay them?

Unpaid internships aren't just a financial burden; they are symptomatic of a deeper failure in our values. If we don't invest in nurturing talent, we can't expect anyone else to invest in the sector's long-term success. We are facing unprecedented challenges and the solutions demand new ideas, diverse perspectives, and relentless questioning of the status quo.

Moreover, the expectation that some people should work for free while others profit is inherently unsustainable. The sector often demands incredible dedication and long hours from those passionate about making a difference – but dedication should be met with fair compensation. It's time to challenge this culture of exploitation and insist that hard work in the name of environmental progress is rewarded, not taken for granted.

By continuing to offer unpaid internships, we undermine our credibility and send a clear unspoken message: we value short-term cost savings over long-term impact – the very impact many of us are claiming we need. If we're truly committed to sustainability and climate resilience, we must first prove that we can sustain our own workforce. Paid internships are a declaration to the world that we are serious about professionalising this sector, bringing it in line with industries that recognise and reward talent.

Investing in paid internships does more than level the playing field – it signals a future-facing, professionalised environment sector. By fostering equitable, well-compensated roles, we show governments, businesses, and investors that we're not just playing at saving the world; we're building a new asset class and a sustainable industry, grounded in fairness and ambition. After all, how can we talk about sustainability if our own practices are fundamentally unsustainable?

Unpaid internships aren't just ethically questionable, they are strategically short sighted. To build the leaders who will navigate the complex challenges of climate change, biodiversity restoration, and sustainable development, we must first invest in them. In the end, the path to a sustainable planet runs through valuing those working tirelessly to secure its future – today's interns and tomorrow's leaders.

On reflection

Sometimes the numbers do the talking, and sometimes, they just leave you speechless.

In 2025, 2,000 remarkable individuals applied for just five internship roles across Oxygen Conservation. That's not a typo – it's a tidal wave of talent. An extraordinary and humbling response that says something powerful about our brand, our mission, and our team. Credit where it's due: this moment belongs to our marketing and people teams, who crafted an offer, a message, and a process that resonated far and wide.

The diversity of applicants was jaw-dropping – we saw PhDs, postgrads, Oxbridge firsts, elite athletes, international performers, and professional musicians. Trail-hardened explorers and deep-thinking academics. It culminated in something truly special: an assessment day that brought the finalists together with our whole team for a shared experience of connection, curiosity, and conversation.

The hosting Estate team orchestrated the day completely unreasonably. Every detail reflected our values and every moment was designed to bring people together in a meaningful, positively challenging way. It wasn't just about who could 'interview well'; it was about who could listen, reflect, contribute, elevate, and lead.

From that magic, we made offers to five phenomenal people. Our intern programme is not a hiring strategy – it's a foundation for the future of the sector, and I love it!

However, here's where this reflection gets uncomfortable. For too long, we've said no to work-experience placements – out of fear, mostly. Fear of criticism, of misunderstanding, of getting it wrong. Fear that offering unpaid experience (even when people are actively asking for it) would open us to accusations of exploitation. Instead, we chose the safe path – rare for us, I appreciate, but in the environment sector especially, this issue comes with a huge amount of emotional baggage.

In doing so, we missed the chance to help people we could – and should – have helped. Not anymore.

In 2025, we made the decision to open our doors to meaningful, well-structured, and strictly limited work-experience opportunities. It's not about replacing paid roles. It's not about free labour. It's about saying yes to people actively seeking to learn, contribute, and understand what this sector really involves.

Here's what we stand by: if we advertise it, it's a job – and it's paid. If someone expectational approaches us asking for work experience, we will consider it if:

- It benefits them more than us
- It is meaningful and managed, never a burden on the team
- It does not exceed one month – beyond that, the work becomes paid
- It leaves the individual better prepared for their next step, wherever that may be

We're not perfect. This is our starting point, but I'm proud that, collectively, the leadership team has created an approach that reflects who we are: a business bold enough to try, honest enough to admit we got it wrong, and committed enough to do better.

You will be able to learn how this develops in our newsletters, on the podcast, or maybe in the next book. For now, this is our simple promise: we're choosing courage over comfort and people over policy, and we're doing it in a way that's 100% Oxygen Conservation.

Warning: What No One Tells You About High Performance

Written March 2025

Oxygen Conservation is a high-performance environment. Many people think they want to work in that kind of space, but few truly understand what it takes. The demands, the pressure, the relentless drive to reinvent not just what you do, but who you are – simply to keep your place in the team. This isn't just about working hard; it's about recalibrating your entire mindset to exist in a space where expectations don't plateau – they escalate.

Knowing who will make it

Several years ago, after appearing on the Extrology podcast (www.extrology.com) with the wonderful Lee Cooper, I was introduced to an incredible founder who had built two businesses from inception to valuations in the hundreds of millions. He was exceptionally kind and loved the concept of Oxygen Conservation. Quietly, calmly, and confidently, he told me he was sure we would be one of the world's first unicorn conservation companies. His only question was whether I knew that half the people in the room with me at that moment wouldn't be there when we got there. Simply put, they wouldn't be able to perform at the highest level.

He was a little surprised when I said I did. Specific people immediately came to mind – good performers who had contributed enormously to the early days of the business, but wouldn't be able to sustain the intensity required at the highest level. It wasn't a question of talent; it was a question of sustainability, resilience, and adaptability.

Some environments are too demanding for long-term participation, and recognising that isn't failure – it's reality for all of us, including me. I was privileged to play international sport for two years. By the third year, my body and my willingness to endure the sacrifices and pain required hadn't improved as fast as the next generation coming through, and I knew that my time had come.

Growth means change

As Oxygen Conservation matures as a business, we're having to say goodbye to some of the people who starred in the earlier chapters of our story, but can't – or aren't willing to – continue making the sacrifices required to perform at this level. The people who build the foundations won't always be the same ones that thatch the roof. It's the natural evolution of a high-performance team.

Imagine an incredible team that rapidly works its way up through the football leagues – like Brighton, for example. How many of the players from the lower division days are realistically ever likely to star in the Premiership or in European competitions?

This isn't offered with criticism or judgment. Instead, it's a sincere thank you to those who made the commitments required for the period that worked for them and their families. However, high performance isn't an environment that is for everyone, and it's certainly not for everyone forever. If you aren't growing, pushing, recalibrating, you'll find yourself watching from the sidelines as the game speeds past you – I remember, because I've done it.

The athlete's parallel

The average career of a professional athlete in the NFL lasts around four years. Why? Because the physical and mental demands are so immense.

Sustained excellence is brutal. The world's best athletes aren't the ones who simply have talent; they are the ones who develop the work and adaptation capacity to reinvent themselves season after season, finding new ways to stay on top and new methods to push the boundaries of what they thought was possible.

If you want a glimpse into the realities of sustaining excellence, listen to James Vowles on the *High Performance* podcast (Hughes and Hughes, 2024). His journey from data analyst to Formula 1 team principal is a masterclass in reinvention, resilience, and the sacrifices required to stay at the top.

In elite sport, the ability to adapt, push boundaries, and embrace discomfort is what separates those who survive from those who thrive. It's no different at Oxygen Conservation, yet still, thousands of people want to be part of this adventure – and that's not hyperbole. We had more than 5,000 applications for roles in 2025 alone. If you were among them, thank you!

It's only fair to share the reality of what it takes to work in a truly high-performance environment. If you want to stay at the top, you'll need to push beyond what you thought was your breaking point; and you *will* break. Then you'll have to decide if you're willing to go faster and further.

The reality of high performance

High performance isn't for everyone, nor is it for everyone forever. Most people aren't prepared to make the sacrifices required to perform at this level. Some who are willing to make them won't sustain it in the long term, and that's OK.

The tools, techniques, ways of working, and people that got you to high performance won't necessarily keep you there – you must constantly reinvest in yourself to find marginal gains. Even the best performers rarely maintain peak performance for long – it's incredibly difficult and demands commitment, resilience, sacrifice, compromise, and selfishness (I understand most people won't like that word, but to any athlete or elite performer, it makes perfect sense).

The bar is always rising. The standard is the standard today, but it will be higher tomorrow. The pressure is immense. In a high-performance environment, you will be surrounded by the best of the best. More will be demanded of you than ever before – not just by your team, but by yourself. You may find the opportunity, the challenge, the freedom, and the support addictive – and that in itself isn't easy to manage.

Some days will be exhilarating. Others will be so demanding that it can feel crushing. There will be moments when you feel unstoppable and moments when you wonder if you can keep going or if you deserve to be here. That's the nature of working at this level. It's not just a job – it's an endurance test.

The opportunity is too big for us to play small

As an organisation that demands high performance, Oxygen Conservation was never meant to be an easy place to work – it can't be. The consequences of failure are too great, and the opportunity to make a positive environmental and social impact is too significant.

Too many people have worked too hard to create the opportunities for the impact that we have now. Too many people have invested everything in making this business a reality – and if you're one of them, thank you. We must take that opportunity forward. We owe it to them. We owe it to ourselves.

The balance of challenge and support

Like a professional sports team, Oxygen Conservation doesn't leave high performers to fend for themselves. We provide coaching, mentorship, and the flexibility needed to keep pushing boundaries without constantly burning out. High performance isn't about running on empty – it's about knowing when to push and when to recover; how to evolve and how to sustain excellence over time.

At Oxygen Conservation, we invest in our people through tailored development programmes, access to industry-leading expertise, and a culture that embraces both challenge and support. We understand that success isn't just about the sprint – it's about having the endurance for the marathon. By ensuring our team has the resources, training, and resilience to keep growing, we build an environment where the best can continue to be their best.

You don't have to do the work – but someone else will, and when they do, they'll bring the hunger, the energy, and the drive that keeps this place electric. Talent might open the door, but it won't hold it open for you. If you want a comfortable ride, there are plenty of other places that will gladly offer you one.

If you want to be challenged, stretched, exhausted, and elated all in the same day, then step forward. The world's first unicorn conservation company isn't going to build itself. Do you want to know if you have what it takes?

On reflection

The New Zealand All Blacks are famous for many things – legendary discipline, relentless hard work, and one non-negotiable rule: *no dickheads*. It's a mindset we share at Oxygen Conservation.

We're building the world's first unicorn conservation company, and that means high standards, no excuses, and zero tolerance for ego. This isn't a place for passengers. It's for those willing to work harder, grow faster, and push further than they thought possible.

If that excites you – if it lights something up inside and makes you want to test the edge of your own potential – then we want to hear from you.

You're Not an Estate Manager? Perfect

Written August 2025

There used to be a stark contrast between our central team at Oxygen Conservation and the talent we were able to attract to work directly on our estates. While our central roles were filled with industry-leading experts in investment, natural capital, marketing, and environmental impact, the estate-based roles lagged far behind. The traditional pipeline for estate managers was all but empty, the few exceptional ones were happy in senior roles at other prominent estates, and the remaining majority were often defined by outdated priorities (hill farming, tenanted agriculture, and/or sporting enterprises) and an approach that simply didn't align with our vision for the future of conservation.

What an Oxygen Conservation estate manager should be

Our early hypothesis was simple: scale. Surely it was about the geographic challenge. Great people can work from anywhere in the UK if the role is remote, but estate management demands proximity – literal boots on the ground.

The deeper we looked, the more broken the pipeline became. Estate management as a concept seemed stuck in an older era – and it showed. We weren't just fishing in a small pond; we were casting into one that had already dried up.

We were wanting and asking for something completely different. Then something brilliant happened. Charles Owen joined the team as head of estate management, and we had the physical embodiment of what an Oxygen Conservation estate manager should be. Slowly, members of our own central team started raising their hands.

'Could I be an estate manager?'

Turns out, when you peel back the prejudices (ours and everyone else's), estate management at Oxygen Conservation is more about entrepreneurialism, people skills, storytelling, logistics, ambition, creating a better future, and just enough audacity, less about clinging to the past and doing what we've always done.

Much like famed football managers Pep Guardiola turning fullbacks into midfielders and Jürgen Klopp creating hybrid wingbacks who could be as impactful in both attack and defence, we were changing the game. We stopped recruiting for the title and started hunting for skills: project management, genuine hospitality, stakeholder engagement, environmental impact, a love of adventure, and most importantly, a passion for a specific place.

This transformation gave our brilliant people team the blueprint they needed. No longer constrained by outdated job titles or descriptions, they could now search for the skills, attributes, and qualities that define an exceptional Oxygen Conservation estate manager, and they did just that. They went out and found them. Individuals with the drive, ambition, and emotional intelligence to lead our estates with vision and integrity.

As a result, while we still get significantly fewer applications for geographically specific roles, the gap that once existed between our central team and our estate team is no longer there. That distinction has vanished. Now? We have estate managers who used to run events, consult on business strategy, create woodland, and compete in elite sport. They've done academic research, led community outreach, managed ecotourism experiences, and yes, planned many weddings. What unites them isn't a CV full of estate names. It's a mindset. A love of nature. An obsessive attention to detail. A thirst for meaning and adventure. A relentless drive to make their estate something incredibly special.

We stopped looking for estate managers – and that's how we found them.

On reflection

I asked our wonderfully talented non-traditional estate managers to reflect on this article. This is what they had to say:

> 'Reading this article, I felt like someone had quietly been watching my old hospitality shifts and decided those skills belonged on an estate. The same love of hosting people, noticing the small details, and doing those extra touches to make guests feel welcome now runs through everything I do as an estate manager at Oxygen Conservation. The "all

day, every day" energy of hospitality has simply become the enjoyable chaos of balancing conservation, ecotourism guests, and visitors while still keeping standards high. What makes it all worthwhile is seeing people's faces light up when they connect with the estate and knowing those moments are shaped by the care happening behind the scenes.'

— Archie Barnes, Mornacott and Leighon Estate Manager

'I don't come from a traditional estate-management background. In fact, I have no previous experience in land management at all. What I do have is a deep passion for wildlife, a determination to challenge old assumptions, and a real desire to help shape the future of conservation.

'My career has been in music and hospitality – worlds that seem completely removed from managing a 12,000-acre Highland estate, but in reality they've equipped me with exactly the traits this role demands. As a musician, progress only comes from hard work, constant practice, and a commitment to learning for the sake of improvement rather than reward. That inner drive to keep pushing forward has shaped how I approach everything. Hospitality, on the other hand, taught me that every detail matters. Whether it's the way cup handles are aligned or ensuring every guest leaves feeling they've had a magical experience, the small things add up to something much bigger. Those principles translate directly into estate management: long hours, an eye for detail on a far larger canvas, and a relentless commitment to improving and evolving.

'Put together, these experiences make me well-suited to the role. As a colleague here likes to say, I want everything perfect – yesterday!'

— Ben Bidmead, Invergeldie Estate Manager

'Embracing the title Manor Farm Estate Manager has been the most unique, diverse learning experience I have ever encountered. Each day blends ecological stewardship, strategic planning, and hands-on problem solving in ways that continually challenge and inspire me. I've developed a deeper respect for land, wildlife, and relationship building while strengthening leadership, adaptability, and decision-making skills. The role has expanded my perspective, reinforced my values, and given me meaningful pride in contributing to long-term environmental protection.'

— Ash Murrell, Manor Farm Estate Manager

'In many ways, the estate manager role mirrors my past work: I get the agenda, the budget, and the timeframe – and I make it happen, solving problems as they come. With the Oxygen Conservation team behind me, there's very little I can't achieve, but nothing has matched the satisfaction and sense of accomplishment this role brings. Instead of working late to deliver a corporate event or renovate someone's home, I'm now putting in the extra hours to transform the land I walk every day.'

— Will Lister, Siblyback Estate Manager

SIX

Scaling The Future: Communities And Connections

Activity is the Antidote for Anxiety

Written September 2025

At the launch of Oxygen Conservation's first book, *Scaling Conservation: The Business of Restoring the Wild,* our team took to the stage for a live Q&A with some of the sharpest minds in the natural capital space. Among the many insightful questions, one has stayed with me.

It came from our parent company's General Counsel, the brilliantly incisive Matt Gingell – a man whose thinking cuts through complexity with disarming clarity. He asked, simply and powerfully: 'How does the Oxygen Conservation team stay so relentlessly optimistic in the face of the climate and biodiversity crises?'

Answering an insightful question

It's a question I haven't stopped thinking about. Here's my best attempt at answering it.

Meaningful action on purpose

Our optimism is grounded in purposeful, meaningful action. It's not a mask; it's a hard-earned belief that the work we do truly matters – ecologically, socially, and economically.

At Oxygen Conservation, anxiety has no room to grow because we're always in motion. Whether we're restoring ecosystems, removing outdated infrastructure, rewetting peatlands, or reimagining landscapes, we act decisively. Movement is medicinal. Action is a core value.

For example, at Dorback in the Cairngorms, we welcomed the local community back to the Estate within twenty-four hours of completing the deal – demonstrating our immediate commitment to delivering environmental and social impact.

Indicators of impact

We aim for irreversible ecological and systemic transformation. When silent landscapes begin to sing again, when degraded areas burst with new life, we know we're doing something right.

For example, At Swineley in the Yorkshire Dales, vole populations exploded following the removal of sheep, drawing back birds of prey and dramatically reshaping local biodiversity in just months.

Learning from the land

Nature isn't our backdrop – it's our collaborator. It challenges our assumptions and teaches us patience. We prioritise being on the ground, observing, listening, and learning. Our results aren't conceptual. They're tangible, messy, and real.

For example, at Esgair Arth on Cardigan Bay in Wales, we freed ancient rainforest from the grip of historic fencing and outdated farming infrastructure – restoring natural processes while planting new woodland.

Earned optimism

Optimism at Oxygen Conservation isn't theoretical – it's built in the field. In the moments where we're drenched, tired, and still smiling because the land is responding.

We've travelled hundreds of thousands of miles, visited a multitude of estates, and walked for days to identify the best opportunities to deliver positive impact and generate a profit as a result, not as the purpose, of what we do.

Scaling people and progress

Every new hire, every estate, every deal, and every acre is proof that scale and impact can coexist. Our people are living, breathing possibilities.

We've created nearly forty new roles across the natural capital economy – blending economists with engineers, data scientists with adventurers – to form an elite, impact-driven group.

Recruiting for the extraordinary

We hire for potential. For vision. For drive. We're looking for those who see the world differently and have the courage to act.

We've worked hard to professionalise the environmental sector through ambition and audacity – attracting almost 2,000 applicants for our intern programme in 2024, and building a pipeline of sector-shaping talent.

From belief to reality

Believing in transformation is one thing. Building it is another. We don't just envision systems change – we execute it.

For example, our premium carbon credits have broken the world record for the highest price paid (£125 per tonne). We've achieved this by committing to quality and refusing to follow the norms of the voluntary carbon market.

Culture in motion

Oxygen Conservation isn't a traditional organisation. It's a movement of highly motivated people aligned in purpose and unreasonable in their commitment to delivery – engage with us and you'll feel it.

For example, our sector-leading *Shoot Room Sessions* podcast invites our team and wider sector to share their honest reflections – embedding transparency and shared learning.

Positivity through performance

Our optimism is forged – not found. It emerges from doing hard things well, together. We are privileged to have access to the landscapes our work is changing for the better, and we spend time in them as a team as often as we possibly can. That connection matters.

Oxygen Conservation isn't an easy place to work – and it's not meant to be. High standards demand constant growth. We've seen good people come and go, but every new recruit raises the bar for the whole team. We only recruit people better than us in a meaningful way.

Driven by purpose

Purpose propels us. It overrides fear, silences hesitation, and fuels action. We're building systems that regenerate nature and redefine value.

We've rejected offers of significant investment and other commercial opportunities because they would have compromised our culture and ability to deliver authentically. Purpose guides every decision.

A working model for the future

We're a prototype. A living, breathing vision of the future of the natural capital company. A fully operational model of what conservation can be when performance, purpose, and delivery align.

This isn't just a narrative. It's a call to action. A challenge to every complacent compromise masquerading as change.

Here's the truth: I'm not even sure we're truly optimistic. We're just too immersed in action, too focused on outcomes, and too privileged to work alongside the most brilliant people I've ever met to think about anything else.

On reflection

As his question was the inspiration for this article, we thought there was no one better than Matt Gingell, General Counsel at Oxygen House, to write the reflection:

This article made me sit with a question I'd never fully articulated: is my response to the crises emotional or operational? And can action, when detached from feedback, turn us into busy fools – moving constantly yet shifting nothing?

What your writing reveals so clearly is that real optimism isn't a mindset at all. It's operational. It's what emerges when the world answers back. Your work restores the forgotten truth that agency for change is a renewable resource. However, agency, like trust, is hard one and easily lost. It seems to me that maintaining operational agency in a poly crisis is the key to maintaining hope and optimising.

Betting on the Wild: How Extreme Athletes, Elite Poker Players, and Oxygen Conservation Turn Risk into Reward

Written November 2025

In a world increasingly feeling the realities of climate and biodiversity collapse, Oxygen Conservation is both a business and a blueprint for using capital to drive positive impact and risk-adjusted returns.

Risk is a reality of what we do and something to be understood, embraced, and ultimately used as a guide to strategic decision making. While many organisations freeze or act defensively in the face of risk, we position it at the centre of our strategy, recognising it, measuring it, mitigating it, and harnessing it.

Our approach to risk management can be traced to years spent in high-risk environments, including, in my case, navigating white-water rapids or paddling a kayak off waterfalls. It's shaped by the mindset of performance athletes, where preparation, decision making under pressure, and measured instinct are non-negotiable. At the same time, it's grounded in data, in numbers, in game theory – where understanding probability, decision trees, and human psychology gives us the edge.

Some say the world's best risk managers are extreme athletes or elite poker players, those with absolute clarity of purpose and acute awareness of consequence. At Oxygen Conservation, we happen to have access to both, and we use that fusion of instinct and intellect to turn risk into opportunity, not an obstacle.

How Oxygen Conservation manages risk

This philosophy doesn't sit on a shelf – it's embedded in how we acquire land, engage communities, and scale nature-based solutions. Oxygen Conservation's unique background allows us to blend boldness with caution, imagination with evidence. From restoring temperate rainforest on Dartmoor to rewilding sheep-depleted uplands in Scotland, every decision we've made has tested the boundaries of what's possible in both conservation and capital, and yet we've flourished. Every estate, every intervention, every stakeholder conversation has strengthened our framework.

How do we do it?

1. A culture of radical transparency

We've institutionalised openness. Our teams are empowered with the full context, not partial information. From our shoot-room-turned-podcast studio to our estate teams equipped with real-time data, we enable every individual to understand, communicate, and access risk.

Mistakes are met not with blame, but with kindness and curiosity. Lessons aren't hidden – they're discussed, debated, written down, and embedded in our DNA. This transparency fosters trust, accelerates learning, and helps ensure we rarely make the same mistake twice.

2. Operational and strategic dual-lens risk framework

Operational risk? That's the daily work – off-road vehicles, excavators, and drones, managed locally, in the field, and by those who know the land best. These risks are contextual and highly specific, often physical and immediate.

Strategic risk? That's the future – how we make decisions that protect and propel our long-term goals. Overseen centrally, it's where we apply our key risk principles, from disciplined decision making to a data-led mindset and a relentless commitment to alignment with mission.

Strategic risks are often harder than operational risks to quantify, but their impact tends to be far greater. Managing them well requires absolute clarity of purpose, ongoing analysis, and a tolerance for ambiguity.

3. Risk scoring meets pragmatism

We use scoring systems, yes, but we also understand their limitations. Numbers don't tell the whole story. They are one lens, powerful but partial.

At Oxygen Conservation, we supplement quantitative analysis with diverse data sources, expert judgment, local knowledge, and the lived experiences of those with perspectives different from our own. This pluralism ensures that we capture nuance, uncover blind spots, and make decisions that are not only statistically sound, but socially and ecologically informed.

As a result, we combine formal risk matrices with a structured hierarchy of control, designating ownership, ensuring regular reviews, and supporting those closest to the risk to manage it best. Importantly, we ensure the scoring process is participatory, drawing on diverse perspectives to avoid blind spots and build consensus.

4. Governance as a competitive advantage

We have developed a 'risk appetite' framework with our exceptional board, which is designed to ensure rapid and precise interaction where risks are escalated for discussion and counsel. Governance, in this context, becomes a tool for acceleration – not constraint. By clearly delineating thresholds for action and escalation pathways, we transform governance into a high-performance mechanism.

The result? We play fast, confidently, and with great clarity – unlocking speed through structure.

5. We use risk as a growth strategy

Where others see risk as a red light, we see it as a prompt to explore further, to ask sharper questions, and to dive deeper into the data. Every estate we acquire is both a calculated risk and a positive investment, backed by rigorous due diligence, strategic intent, and a broad understanding of ecosystem dynamics.

An illustration of this was our acquisition of the Invergeldie Estate in Perthshire, which was completed within four weeks of our first viewing and added more than 11,000 acres to the portfolio in record time. This wasn't just luck; it was the product of disciplined risk management, a powerful demonstration of how our framework builds confidence, acceleration, and impact.

One of my key learnings from the wonderful book *Thinking in Bets* by Annie Dukes (2018), a world-class poker player, is that all decisions are part skill and part luck, and we will never know the exact balance of the two. Annie also teaches the importance of not assuming good decisions lead to good outcomes; they merely increase the likelihood of a positive outcome occurring. Every decision then becomes a bet on a different version of the future.

6. An integrated always-on system

We're integrating risk management with data from across our portfolio – combining people, ecological, finance, and operations data into a single system. This is not about compliance. It's about performance. About spotting trends early. Acting faster. Moving from reactive to predictive.

We're also investing in remote data acquisition, drone technology, AI-powered analytics, and continuing to enhance our approach to proprietary data modelling to further increase our situational awareness. We're building a dynamic, living risk system, accessible to those who need the information most and can best use it to make decisions.

7. Learning through reflection and iteration

Risk management isn't static; it's an evolving and moving target. That's why we build feedback loops into every aspect of our operation. We hold cross-functional reviews, post-project debriefs, and scenario planning exercises to improve our approach. These aren't one-off exercises – they are embedded rituals that help us stay responsive and resilient.

A great example of this is our approach to wildfire risk assessment. We engaged a leading expert to properly assess wildfire risk in a complex landscape where historic management dictated that burning of the hillside was once a common practice. In stopping this practice to improve the ecological integrity of the landscape, we needed to fully understand any unintended consequences.

Working with a wildfire risk specialist helped us to generate a robust set of procedures and build a network of collaborators to manage the ever-increasing risk of wildfire. Now, we are in conversations with international experts who use advanced satellite and weather telemetry data to model the risk of wildfire, run scenarios to strategically place firebreaks that will significantly reduce the risk to our growing natural capital assets, and consider early warnings of increased risk and perhaps, in future, even fire identification itself.

We also run internal risk audits, simulate edge-case scenarios, and encourage every team member to flag emergent patterns or anomalies in real-time. This decentralised alertness means that our strategy is shaped not just by leadership, but by everyone embedded in our landscapes, systems, and processes.

This reflexivity is vital in a fast-changing sector where yesterday's insight might – well, almost certainly will – become today's risk. By continuously updating our understanding and adapting our approach, we stay ahead of risk not by trying to eliminate it, but by learning to navigate it with confidence and agility.

Risk management in the market for natural capital

As we seek to professionalise conservation, we recognise our responsibility to elevate risk management standards across the natural capital economy. Our commitment to sharing our approach isn't about claiming perfection – it's about helping shape a smarter, more resilient future. We believe that transparency, reflection, and collaboration are key to unlocking the true potential of nature-based solutions at scale.

That's why we share our learnings through publications, partnerships, podcasts, and policy dialogues. It's why we open our doors to those bold enough to challenge convention and curious enough to build something better. We want to inspire others to view risk not as a liability, but as an invitation to lead with courage and clarity, and we want to keep learning too – by listening, evolving, and iterating in public.

Ultimately, professionalising risk management isn't just about protecting against downside – it's about expanding the upside for everyone. That's how we make the market for natural capital. That's why we'll never stop improving the way we think about and act on risk.

This article was based on an internal paper original led by Dave Keir (head of operations) and our own risk management expert. Dave is an engineer with experience of working and leading teams in the most highly regulated and high-consequence industries on the planet.

The article was also inspired by ideas contained within the books *Thinking in Bets* by Annie Dukes (2018) and *Black Box Thinking* by Matthew Syed (2025).

On reflection

I asked Adam Franks, Chair of Blue and White Capital, one of our wonderful investors, to write the reflection. His mentorship has been extraordinary, and his experience of managing risk is unmatched.

As a lifelong investor drawn to the edge where risk meets opportunity, I found Betting on the Wild both familiar and compelling. It captures a truth too often missed: risk isn't a hazard to hide from, but the ground on which new value is made.

Oxygen Conservation's blend of transparency, operational rigour and strategic risk-taking is precisely what will professionalise natural capital. Like at the card table, the aim isn't to banish uncertainty – it's to price it, size it, and play it well.

What's at stake is more than capital: it's mainstreaming natural capital to build a more resilient future.

The Knight's Dilemma: Positive Intent and Unintended Consequences

Written July 2025

Lately, I've found myself drawn to the idea of consequences – not the ones we plan for, but the ones that arrive uninvited. Unintended consequences are the echoes of our decisions, the shadows we don't always see until they fall. They don't ask permission. They just happen – and whether we acknowledge it or not, they will usually affect someone, often negatively.

This realisation didn't surface in a strategy session or on a wind-swept hillside in Scotland. It began with chess.

Chess, with its rules and rituals, is a beautifully structured game, but beneath its order lies a metaphor for complexity. Each piece follows a code, each move sets off a cascade of outcomes.

Consider the knight: agile, unpredictable, unorthodox. You deploy it with intent, seeing a strategic gain. From your vantage point, it's the right move, but that same success will result in someone else's loss or discomfort.

If your judgment was flawed, the unintended consequences might be yours.

This is the reality of leadership at Oxygen Conservation. We act with purpose and positive intent. We acquire land, restore ecosystems, ease pressures on landscapes, reintroduce species, and install infrastructure like wind turbines. These decisions are grounded in evidence and driven by data, but every single one sends ripples through complex ecological and human systems. While many of those ripples are regenerative, sometimes the exact same ripples inevitably disrupt these same systems.

It's all about perspective

Unintended consequences are not failures – they are features of complexity. Sometimes, the fallout is serendipitous: a blocked ditch brings back a wetland alive with biodiversity. Other times, tension emerges: a decision to control deer populations in line with national policy sparks friction with traditional sporting interests. Both outcomes come from the same action with the same positive intent, but are perceived in starkly different ways depending on your position or perspective.

Perspective, then, becomes not a luxury, but a necessity, because no single viewpoint can reveal the whole picture. What we see from the summit is not what someone else sees from the shoreline. Without multiple vantage points, we operate in narrowness – and in conservation, that narrowness risks repeating the mistakes of the past under a different name.

True perspective demands curiosity and humility – the ability to recognise that our models are incomplete, our knowledge is imperfect. It asks us to consider, with genuine empathy, how others might perceive and receive the decisions we make. Often, it means recognising that we'll never fully understand someone else's experience – and acting with care anyway.

That's why at Oxygen Conservation, while we work fast, we think about everything – we discuss and debate with subject matter experts. Nothing is done by accident. We never act without purpose. Every move is backed by data, by scenario testing, by consideration of consequence. We simulate backlash. We anticipate conflict. We design not for perfection, but for adaptability and impact.

Pushing the knight

Returning to the knight, you could keep it tucked away, safe on the back row of the board, pushing pawns in cautious increments. That's what many have done, making little impact and waiting for someone else to act. Many still do, but that's not why the knight exists.

It's not what we do either. At Oxygen Conservation, we're here to make intentional strategic moves in service of a larger goal: to restore ecosystems, regenerate landscapes, and redefine conservation.

Action creates risk and weight. The weight of knowing that we will inevitably cause effects we didn't intend. That someone, somewhere, will be impacted in ways we didn't foresee. That the stories we tell ourselves about doing good will sometimes be tested by the realities others experience – although often these are only contradictions and compromises. That's the reality of our world.

This is the price of leadership in a sector that for too long has prized tradition over transformation. Apathy over action. Doing what's always been done is no longer enough. Safe moves might avoid scrutiny, but they won't help save the planet. We must act boldly, transparently, and with the courage to take responsibility – not just for our intentions, but for our outcomes.

We ask:

- What if your best move disrupts someone else?
- What if your gain comes at a cost to someone?
- What if the planet's gain comes at a cost to you?
- What if doing the right thing still comes with criticism?

Would you push the knight? We would.

Now the board is set. It's your turn. The decision is yours. What move will you make?

On reflection

This reflection comes from Dave Keir, Oxygen Conservation's head of operations.

I met Rich in January 2007 at university, which means I've now had nearly two decades of front-row seats at the same pattern playing out again and again: he makes the move.

Sometimes it's a brilliant one. Sometimes it's a difficult one. Sometimes it's a move that only makes sense once you've seen what it unlocks two or three steps later, but the core of him has been steady throughout.

Rich has an unreasonable bias towards action, and a stubbornly positive intent behind it. He'll have 1,000 conversations that lead nowhere and still wake up the next day ready to have another one, because he genuinely believes there might be a way to help, or a piece of advice that changes the shape of a problem, or a partnership worth taking a swing at. That persistence isn't noise; it's how momentum gets built in a world where most people would rather wait for certainty than risk being wrong.

I'm one of the early examples of that instinct. One of his first moves, long before Oxygen Conservation existed, was simply taking an interest in an eighteen-year-old engineering student who was equal parts argumentative and sarcastic. He didn't have to. There was no upside for him in it, but he did it anyway, in his own unique way: curious, generous with his time, nudging me into bigger conversations and wider horizons than I was aiming at then. I don't think either of us would have framed it as anything significant at the time, but looking back, I realise it quietly changed a lot for me. It was also probably the first clue I got that his positive intent isn't performative. It's reflex.

In fairness, early Rich made his moves with a bit more swagger. He was cocky and brash in the way only a bright twenty-something can be, convinced that if he pushed the knight hard enough, the board would rearrange itself in his favour. Over time, that edge hasn't disappeared; it's been refined. The drive is still there, but it's paired with clearer thinking and better timing. The moves are less about speed for its own sake and more about speed with purpose. There's a calmness to the way he thinks now, not in the sense of being cautious, but in being precise. Clear about why we're doing something, clear about what it might set in motion, and clear that if we're going to do this work properly, we have to be willing to hold complexity in both hands at once.

This is why the knight is fitting. Rich has always loved that piece. We have played enough chess for me to know he leans on it a little too much, which makes him easier to beat than he would like to admit. Still, the instinct is right. The knight's move can change the board.

The article is a reminder that every such move sends ripples. Some heal, some jar, most do both depending on where you are standing. The job is to see as much as we can, listen hard when we miss something, and own what happens next.

Take this as my encouragement before you read on. Rich will keep pushing the knight. He always has. The question is whether you will do the same, with the same clarity and courage.

Community: Not Where You Are – What You Do

Written July 2025

Community: a word laden with nostalgia; an illusion of unity and shared purpose that we long for but rarely find. We speak of it in reverent tones, reminiscing about a distant past where tight-knit neighbourhoods and collective responsibility were the norm. Does this romanticised version of community still exist, or are we clinging to a myth lost in time?

What do we mean by community?

For many, community is rooted in a deep love for a specific place – a town, a landscape, a set of familiar names and faces tied to geography. Sadly, I don't share that connection. My childhood was not pleasant. Certainly not one I wished to remain bound to, and I took every opportunity to move forwards – to university, to jobs across the UK, to building something better than I was given. Home for me is not a place; it is where my wife, children, and team are. My friendships and collaborations span time zones and continents, enabled by technology, the nature of our work, and a drive for lifelong learning and improvement.

I've met some incredible people who feel tied to a particular place, who carry an unshakable love for a landscape or a town, sometimes even a city. Occasionally, I wish I felt the same. There's something deeply grounding about feeling tethered to a specific place, a physical anchor for identity and belonging, and yet I've come to appreciate the flexibility that detachment offers – how it has allowed me to be open to new places, people, and ideas. In many ways, this fluidity has shaped my vision of a broader, more inclusive kind of community – one not limited by borders, but expanded by shared values and goals.

Then I remind myself that for many, especially the next generation, this kind of belonging is becoming rarer. The world has changed, and so too has our sense of community.

Consensus

Historically, we have thought of communities as unified entities speaking with a single voice. In reality, that voice is usually the loudest, the self-appointed spokesperson who often does not represent the whole. Public interest or self-interest masquerading as the collective will. Community-washing, if you will – the illusion of consensus when, in fact, no such agreement exists. Democratically elected groups or those occupying lesser public sector roles are largely ignored, rarely supported, and almost always disliked as they are held to standards no one can hope to achieve.

This is particularly evident in rural land debates. Small landowners and crofters, for instance, may present themselves as the many, as the grassroots voices against larger conservation efforts or land restoration initiatives. It's essential to acknowledge their lived experiences, histories, and the sense of place that informs their perspectives. These views matter, deeply. However, it's also worth recognising that they represent just one part of a broader picture.

The many include not just those who live locally, but also those of us contributing through our taxes and pensions – resources that could be mobilised for large-scale environmental restoration. The real community, then, extends beyond geographic proximity to everyone invested – financially, ecologically, and socially – in a better future for people and wildlife.

Engagement

Much like our outdated consensus structures – a thirteenth-century operating system trying to govern a twenty-first-century world – our engagement and consultation models are fundamentally flawed. Why is it that those making proposals regarding an area are required to consult those who live in arbitrary proximity rather than those with expertise, long-term vision, and broader interests?

Imagine if every major decision operated this way. Instead of legal frameworks and professional governance, we'd defer to the whims of the nearest neighbour as judge, jury, and executioner. This absurdity would never hold in sectors like healthcare, engineering, or technology, yet we persist with it in matters of land use and conservation. Should we consult a specialist surgeon or the person who happens to live at the end of the road? I'll let you decide the next time you're unwell.

If traditional communities are the ideal self-sustaining entities they claim to be, why do so many young people leave? Opportunity, ambition, progress – these rarely thrive in stagnation. The reality is, many of these communities resist change, holding onto past structures that no longer serve the very people they claim to be protecting.

Nostalgia is a poor substitute for a viable future. If you don't believe me, just ask the young people in your community.

Does community still exist?

Perhaps, but not in the way the majority think. People now belong to many communities simultaneously, shaped by identity, profession, interests, and global connectivity rather than mere geography. I believe in libertarianism and support people's freedom of choice as long as it doesn't harm others, and that includes the communities a person chooses to identify with, or not.

It's taken me a while to realise this, but at Oxygen Conservation, we've been fortunate to help build a new type of community – one that spans more than 20,000 people across our social channels, writing, podcasts, ecotourism experiences, and speaking engagements. We've had podcast listeners write to share how the episodes inspired them to change career paths or get directly involved in conservation – one of our new estate managers did exactly that. With more than 10,000 people applying to be part of Oxygen Conservation, it's clear that this community is not just engaged, but ready to roll up its sleeves and help us Scale Conservation.

This is a community not bound by postcode or parish, but by shared purpose and passion. A network of people who believe in the natural capital economy, who are committed to delivering positive environmental and social impact, and who recognise that business is our best shot at driving meaningful, lasting change. Perhaps the challenge is not preserving an outdated model of community, but redefining what collective action looks like in a modern world – where belonging is fluid, expertise matters, and the voices of the many (wherever they come from) extend far beyond those who simply happen to live next door and would rather nothing at all changed, even for the better.

Many people who live near our estates care passionately about the land, its history, and its future – and we respect that. A noted leader in environment finance visited Manor Farm in Norfolk, and covertly asked everyone he met about Oxygen Conservation. He was delighted to share with us that the local community was glowing with praise about the work we do to help people and wildlife. However, we must also accept that positive change often challenges the status quo. This isn't about undermining local voices; it's about expanding the conversation to include those who might otherwise be excluded, despite being meaningfully invested in the outcomes.

If community is no longer confined to postcode and tradition, then we must embrace its evolution as both a challenge and an opportunity. The future belongs to communities of action – those united not by proximity, but by shared values, vision, and the courage to build something better.

Whether you're next door to one of our estates or following from afar, if you care about people and planet, you're already part of this movement. Community isn't where you are. It's what you do. Together, we can choose to redefine it – not as a myth of the past, but as a mission for the future.

On reflection

The above article and the one that follows were written only months apart and demonstrate how I use the process of writing to help share my understanding of our work and our world. The term community has often been weaponised against Oxygen Conservation in many of the things we try to do for people and wildlife, but over time I've learned to think about it in a very different way.

Beyond Borders: The Community Oxygen Built

Written December 2025

Community is one of those words that most people think they understand. For centuries, it was easy enough: a community was the collection of people you could see from your front door, the neighbours you nodded to on your way to market, the congregation that filled the church pews on Sunday. Community had edges: hedge-rows, parish boundaries, the limits of how far you could walk in a day.

Today, community no longer obeys fences, footpaths, or even families. It doesn't exist only in village halls or around parish noticeboards. It lives in podcasts and LinkedIn posts, in shared ambition and exchanged ideas.

At Oxygen Conservation, we are living proof of that evolution. We've just broken 10,000 followers on LinkedIn and passed 100,000 YouTube views for *The Shoot Room Sessions*. It's an overwhelming reminder that so many people care, and I feel humbled and grateful beyond words by that signal. It tells me that the community we're building stretches far beyond the twelve estates we manage, from Cornwall to the Cairngorms, from the Welsh coast to Norfolk. Our community doesn't end at the edges of our land – it extends across oceans, into homes, workplaces, and imaginations all over the world.

From estates to ecosystems

When we buy land, we do it to restore, regenerate, and reimagine what's possible for nature in the UK. Leighon, Mornacott, Dorback, and Esgair Arth – these names have become the chapters in our story of Scaling Conservation, but the land is only the canvas. The true art is what happens when people gather around that work.

On our estates, we've invited in communities. Sometimes literally by opening gates, hosting school groups, or welcoming walkers back onto landscapes long since closed. Sometimes metaphorically by sharing our work in radical transparency, publishing first drafts of ideas, and inviting feedback even when we know it might sting. We will listen, even if we don't always agree.

That attitude has built trust, and trust is the foundation of every real community.

Digital doors wide open

When we turned our shoot room into a podcast studio, we closed the doors to the sporting enthusiasts who once visited our estates annually, and opened them to a new kind of community – viewers and fans of the show who now join us weekly in their thousands. We didn't do this to become broadcasters; we did it because we knew storytelling had to become part of conservation.

If the natural capital economy is the fastest game on earth, then we need a commentary team to match. *The Shoot Room Sessions* has become that voice: a place where we share not just polished strategies, but honest doubts, difficult trade-offs, and the behind-the-scenes thinking that most businesses hide.

Global community for local impact

One of the most surprising, and frankly humbling, aspects of our growth has been the international attention. The USA has become a particular hotspot of interest. Maybe it's the scale of landscapes there. Maybe it's the culture of backing bold ideas. Ultimately, it's perhaps not such a surprise – our love of American sport and tech startups means our brand often speaks more naturally to USA culture than to the UK.

Whatever the reason, we now find ourselves in dialogue with investors, ecologists, and entrepreneurs across the Atlantic who want to learn from what we're doing and, increasingly, to invest in it. That's community too. Not in the old sense of borrowing sugar from your neighbour, but in the modern sense of shared ambition. The ambition to make conservation not just possible, but profitable. To prove that protecting nature can compete with the best ideas in Silicon Valley, the sharpest deals in the City of London, or the boldest plays on Wall Street.

Pride in the people

If there's one thing I feel most proud of, it's not the acres acquired or the records set for carbon credit prices. It's the people who make up this community.

The Oxygen Conservation teams themselves – recruited with care, trained like elite athletes, challenged and supported in equal measure – are the beating heart of our work. Around them, a wider circle has formed: our podcast listeners, our LinkedIn network, our investors, our neighbours, critics, collaborators, and even our fiercest detractors. They are all part of the same ecosystem. Some cheer us on, some push us harder, some call us out, but every one of them keeps us sharp, honest, and focused.

Community isn't always comfortable, but it is always necessary.

Redefining what community means

I sometimes think about how odd it would sound to a landowner 100 years ago if I told them their estate would one day host a community that exists online, stretches across continents, and measures its engagement not in cups of tea, but in podcast downloads or LinkedIn interactions. Yet here we are.

The myth of community is that it needs a shared geography. The truth is that it needs a shared story. At Oxygen Conservation, our story is one of urgency, ambition, and belief. Urgency because the biodiversity and climate crises are accelerating. Ambition because we aim to manage a billion pounds of natural capital by 2030. Belief because we know conservation can scale if it stops apologising for wanting to compete. That story has resonated, and in so doing, it has built a community.

Looking forward

Crossing milestones like 10,000 followers, 100,000 views, and 1,000,000 interactions is energising, but they're just markers on a longer journey. What excites me most is imagining where this community can go next. How do we use this platform not just to celebrate success, but to accelerate action? How do we turn attention into more acres, likes into better livelihoods, followers into fellow adventurers on the road to a wilder, better future.

We talk often about Scaling Conservation. That also means scaling a community. Every acre restored is an invitation. Every podcast episode is a door opened. Every social post is a signal to anyone, anywhere, who wants to be part of something bigger.

On reflection

I've always found the idea of community strangely difficult. Maybe that's because I never stayed in one place long enough to call it home. Maybe it's because, like so many people who grew up a little bruised by childhood, I believed belonging was something that happened to other people. Community was something I watched from the edges, never something I felt part of.

This article forced me to confront something unexpected. Somewhere along the way, without fully realising it, Oxygen Conservation built a community. Not the kind I grew up imagining, with village greens and familiar faces at the same kitchen tables, but a community of ambition, curiosity, challenge, and care. A community that stretches far beyond borders, job titles, or postcodes. A community built around a mission so big that people want to lean in, connect, and contribute to it.

What surprised me most is how deeply this community has come to matter to me. The team I work with every day. The people who follow our work from thousands of miles away. The listeners who tune in each week. The critics who push us.

The investors who back us. The ecologists who advise us. The neighbours who welcome us. The apprentices who tell us hard truths. They're not just an audience. They're part of us.

Maybe this is what community looks like when you didn't grow up feeling like you had one. It's not something you inherit. It's something you build. Something that forms around shared belief, not shared childhoods. Something shaped by purpose rather than postcode.

What I've realised is this: community doesn't have to feel like home in the traditional sense to feel like belonging. Maybe for people like me, who never felt rooted in one place, belonging comes through movement, mission, and momentum. Through building something meaningful, surrounded by people who care deeply enough to join you.

The truth is that Oxygen Conservation hasn't just restored landscapes. It's restored something for me personally too. A sense of connection I never expected to find. A network of people who believe in what we're trying to do. A shared story that binds us in ways hedgerows and parish lines never could.

I didn't grow up knowing what community meant. Now, standing in the middle of this one, I finally do, and it's one of the most unexpected and meaningful parts of my journey.

Ecotourism: Opening the Gateway to Wild Places

Written September 2025

At Christmas 2024, we opened the doors to the wonderful Drum Lodge, at Dorback in the Cairngorms, for a family to spend the holidays in the heart of one of the most exciting environmental projects in Britain. Imagine a fire crackling as snow drifts past the window, wild landscapes stretching in every direction, and the chance to wake up each morning inside the most incredible living conservation story.

Why ecotourism matters

Ecotourism is increasingly one of the most important parts of our work – so much so it exerts a disproportionate influence on what we do, how we do it, and how everyone engages with Oxygen Conservation. It amplifies the outcomes of conservation, strengthens partnerships, and broadens the reach of our storytelling. Each visitor interaction with nature – whether a walk in the hills, a swim in a river, or a quiet evening spent under the stars – generates ripples that extend far beyond the immediate experience. Visitors often leave with a renewed sense of purpose and an inclination to advocate for and invest in conservation.

At its foundation, ecotourism is about accessibility, enjoyment, and restorative time spent in nature. It shifts people from passive spectators to active participants, immersed in landscapes alive with bees, butterflies, birds, and the quiet rhythms of ecosystems in recovery. It reminds us that nature is not just something to be admired at a distance, but something to be lived, breathed, and carried with us back into our everyday lives.

These encounters build connections of immense value. For investors, they illustrate conservation's tangible outcomes in ways no data model ever could; for visitors (who are sometimes also investors), they create deeply personal emotional bonds. Ecotourism is temporal as well as spatial: it evokes nostalgia for childhood memories of richer natural worlds while projecting hope for ecological futures that are possible once again.

Importantly, ecotourism is about togetherness. It is rarely experienced alone. Families, couples, and groups of friends carry these moments into their shared histories. An early sunrise or a walk through a rewilded valley becomes more than a fleeting event; it becomes part of collective memory. These are the stories retold at dinner tables, in shared moments, and across generations, seeding conservation.

Ecotourism and our values

Ecotourism mirrors the very values that created Oxygen Conservation. At its core, it is about environment, impact, adventure, and togetherness. These are the guiding principles that shape everything we do. To spend time on our estates is not just to visit spaces and places we have created and curated – it is to step into our story, to share in the ambition, and to feel the pulse of landscapes that are recovering and thriving.

Every visit is an act of participation. When you walk through ancient woodlands, cross restored peatlands, or listen to curlews returning to valleys long quiet, you are experiencing not only the recovery of ecosystems, but the expression of our purpose. Ecotourism offers people a chance to live those values alongside us: to adventure into wild places, to witness real impact, and to build moments of togetherness that strengthen the collective bond between them and the planet. It transforms conservation from something abstract into something intimate, immersive, and unforgettable.

The emotional gateway

Even before a guest arrives, the anticipation of ecotourism can trigger a positive response. It is perceived as a guilt-free form of leisure: restorative, meaningful, and aligned with personal values. Anticipation itself becomes a form of joy and reflection. Families imagine the walks they will take, the wildlife they might glimpse, and the time they will spend together, away from the hustle, bustle, and noise of daily life.

Ecotourism's power lies in tangibility. Data and reports may persuade some, but lived experience persuades nearly everyone. Walking through recovering woodlands, smelling the damp earth of a peat bog, or hearing the return of bird species provides an unparalleled authenticity. It is conservation that can be touched, heard, smelt, felt, and remembered.

For many, ecotourism represents the first time they pause to listen to nature's subtler conversations – the rustle of grasses in a rewilded meadow, the quiet drip of water through sphagnum moss, or the far-off call of stag on the hill. These pauses inspire reflection on how they live, consume, and interact with the world beyond the estate. In this way, ecotourism's influence extends outward – into homes, communities, and workplaces, gently reshaping choices and values.

A rising global demand

Market trends confirm what we observe on the ground: demand for ecotourism is increasing, and rapidly. Globally, it is among the fastest-growing segments of travel. Visitors are not only looking for restorative experiences for themselves, but also for activities that contribute positively to ecosystems and communities. People want their leisure time to matter, to leave a trace not of harm, but of healing.

In the UK, this appetite is particularly pronounced. Increasingly, individuals are seeking local or domestic experiences rather than long-haul travel. This behavioural change not only lowers carbon footprints, but also bolsters the economic rationale for domestic conservation and restoration projects. Ecotourism is, therefore, both an ethical choice and an economic driver. It underpins investment in natural capital, creates green jobs, and supports rural economies that will continue to struggle in the transition away from traditional land use.

For our organisation, ecotourism is not an add-on. It is integral to Scaling Conservation. Each estate must be a place where people can witness and participate in recovery, because if they cannot feel it, they will not fight for it – and without their advocacy, these gains cannot be sustained. Ecotourism transforms visitors into ambassadors and investors, expanding our reach and strengthening our resilience.

A call to action for the sector

For organisations engaged in landscape management, conservation, or restoration, omitting ecotourism from your strategy could be a profound oversight. Beyond generating revenue, it provides the emotional and cultural engagement necessary for long-term success. Without it, projects risk invisibility and diminished support (from both near and far). A restored valley unseen, a peat bog unvisited, or a woodland unheard is vulnerable; ecotourism ensures these landscapes have defenders far beyond their boundaries.

Ecotourism is the connective tissue between ecological processes and human understanding. It converts abstract statistics into lived experiences and transforms restored landscapes into personal legacies. It renders conservation not only viable, but also desirable. It is the spark that turns environmental progress into cultural momentum.

For the environmental sector, this is not about survival alone. It is about establishing resilience, credibility, and relevance. By embedding ecotourism, we broaden conservation's audience, deepen its impact, and ensure its future.

The greatest risk we face is, therefore, perhaps not apathy, but invisibility. Ecotourism brings conservation and the environment into the light – be it from the sun or stars.

When the first family spent their Christmas at Drum Lodge, they were doing more than enjoying a seasonal retreat. They were stepping directly into the evolving future of conservation – a future where landscapes are not locked away, but opened, shared, and cherished. They embodied the principle that conservation is not only a responsibility, but also a privilege and a joy.

That is the essence of ecotourism: to create memories that endure, to ignite collective movements, and to demonstrate that nature, once experienced directly, becomes impossible to ignore. It is both a gift and a challenge: a gift of wonder and togetherness, and a challenge to return home changed, ready to live differently and fight for the future of the wild places we hold dear.

On reflection

Some places don't just sit on a map – they stay with you long after you visit. The Lakes at Manor Farm in Norfolk was one of those rare places. A hidden corner of the estate where time felt slower, lighter, and somehow more honest.

When we first reopened the Lakes after our acquisition, we weren't just launching an ecotourism venture. We were opening a door. Inviting people in. Saying come and see what we see – the beauty in stillness, the wildness in softness, the quiet power of nature doing its work.

People came. They came with children and stories and celebrations. They came to reconnect. They came back again, and again, and again. Many of our guests became part of the place, returning so often it felt as though the Lakes were keeping a guestbook written in memory rather than ink.

The team who carried this chapter did something remarkable. They took on an inherited business and didn't just run it. They lifted it. Evolved it. Polished it into an award-winning experience worthy of the land it sat upon. Record visitor numbers. Record revenues. Record smiles. They made magic in a place already half-magic to begin with.

However, nature teaches us the truth whether we want to hear it or not, and the truth here was simple. Beautiful things aren't always sustainable things. No matter how many guests we welcomed, no matter how efficiently we operated, the cost of running the Lakes grew faster than any price we could fairly charge. Cleaning alone became an adversary we couldn't outpace.

Because Oxygen Conservation is a business built on innovation, not nostalgia, we must listen when the land and the numbers whisper the same message. Try things. Learn. Respond quickly. Not cling to what no longer works.

With a heavy heart and a clear mind, we decided not to reopen the Lakes at Manor Farm in 2026.

There's grief in writing that sentence. The kind that catches for a moment, because this wasn't just glamping. It wasn't tents and timber and check-ins. It was connection. It was community. It was thousands of tiny human moments stitched together by the landscape.

Grief is a sign that something mattered, and the Lakes mattered deeply. They mattered because ecotourism sits at the beating heart of what we do – making estates places for people, not just places on paper. They mattered because they created meaningful local jobs and opportunities. Because they let people touch nature, not as an abstract idea, but as a lived, tangible experience.

They mattered because they taught us. Quickly. Sharply. Honestly.

They taught us that some parts of the portfolio are chapters – not destinations. They taught us that other models, such as our built-property ecotourism at Mornacott, Dorback, and Invergeldie, can soar even higher, generating record revenues while scaling sustainably.

What now for the Lakes? We let the water rest. We breathe. We listen, and we begin imagining the next chapter for this special corner of Manor Farm. Not with haste. Not with nostalgia. With respect. With curiosity. With the same ambition we bring to everything we do.

The Lakes are not ending. They're pausing. Waiting for the right idea, the right purpose, the right partner, the right moment to bloom again in a new form. To every guest who returned – thank you. You became part of this place's story. To Ashlee, Mel, and Alex – your work here is imprinted on the landscapes and the hearts and minds of everyone who visited this special place. The Lakes were beautiful because you made them so.

And to the Lakes themselves – thank you for letting us borrow your magic for a while. This is a farewell. But not a goodbye.

SEVEN

Scaling The Future: Innovation And Imagination

What if Unicorns Roam in Peatlands: Investing in Nature's Next Billion-Dollar Frontier

Written June 2025

An unexpected email landed, inviting us to speak with the senior leadership team of a major financial institution and share a little about our work and the lessons we've learned along the way. Several weeks later, after we'd walked them through our model, projects, and impact, the managing director leaned back in his chair, paused thoughtfully, and said, 'This must be what it felt like when people first heard of Google.'

At the time, it felt like an incredible compliment, but looking back, I realise it reflected a growing realisation that natural capital markets could scale with the same velocity and transformative power as the early internet. The feeling in that room wasn't just curiosity, but conviction about the future.

Welcome to the green inflection point

Picture the year 1994. You're in a meeting where someone introduces the concept of a decentralised data-driven network poised to revolutionise every industry. Most people dismiss the idea. A few crazy ones, the misfits and the rebels, pay attention. Three decades later, those few have helped build trillion-dollar technology giants.

We now stand at a similar crossroads, but this time, the pitch is even more ambitious: forests function as carbon data centres, peatlands serve as natural cloud storage, and ecosystems form the essential infrastructure of tomorrow. What if climate change isn't just an existential threat, but the greatest unrealised economic opportunity of our time? Then, conservation isn't a financial drain – it's a high-growth sector, offering substantial returns on investment, meaningful positive impact, and massive scalability.

In this new era of climate urgency, nature is emerging as the next Silicon Valley.

From altruism to asset class: The evolution of conservation

Historically, conservation has been perceived as philanthropic – important, yet economically irrelevant. That perception is now outdated. Natural capital, which encompasses the quantifiable value of ecosystems and biodiversity, is entering mainstream financial markets. Carbon credits, biodiversity units, and water quality credits have become tradable commodities.

This shift is backed by real financial momentum. Norway's sovereign wealth fund, valued at $1.6 trillion, now assesses nature-related risk across 96% of its portfolio. Institutions like BlackRock are tracking biodiversity exposure. Climate Asset Management has secured over $1 billion to invest directly in environmental restoration, and here in the UK, Oxygen Conservation has built a Natural Capital Portfolio valued at more than £200m.

This is the hostile takeover of ecological collapse, a chance to disrupt the climate crisis and profit as a result.

Ecosystems as infrastructure: Forests, peatlands, and wetlands

Think about digital infrastructure. Billions have been spent building the internet: server farms, fibre optic cables, and satellites. Now, as we face the environmental crises of the twenty-first century, we require infrastructure that can regulate climate, store carbon, and ensure access to clean water. Fortunately, nature already provides this, but until now, we've never paid the bill.

Forests, peatlands, and wetlands provide these essential environmental services. These natural systems function like living infrastructure, improving over time and delivering both ecological and economic value. Instead of depreciating like human-made assets, they appreciate through restoration and thoughtful stewardship.

Oxygen Conservation manages over 50,000 acres of UK land; land that integrates carbon sequestration, renewable energy, habitat creation, and community benefit (homes and jobs in rural communities). These are high-performing environmental assets.

Nature as a prime investment class

Regulatory frameworks are reinforcing this shift. The EU's Corporate Sustainability Reporting Directive

(CSRD) and the TNFD are embedding nature into financial and compliance systems.

Simultaneously, market expectations are rising. Consumers are demanding authenticity and transparency over any suggestion of greenwashing. Corporations are seeking credits and metrics backed by science, integrity, and transparency. The result is a consolidation towards high-integrity, high-quality nature markets.

To meet this demand, we developed the Oxygen Conservation Carbon Curve, a pricing model that forecasts significant rises in high-quality carbon credits (and, in time, nature credits) aligned with project quality and market maturity. Importantly, the carbon market has laid the groundwork for the emerging nature markets. Systems for verification, pricing, and trading developed for carbon are now being adapted to accommodate biodiversity and ecosystem services, creating a scalable framework for natural capital investment.

Innovation beyond digital: Conservation tech and strategy

Technological innovation is beginning to reshape conservation in promising ways. Blockchain technology is being tested to improve transparency in nature credit transactions. AI is showing potential for supporting real-time biodiversity monitoring. Satellite imagery is enabling early efforts in ecosystem assessment at scale. While these tools are still developing, they hint at a future where environmental restoration is powered by digital precision and data-driven decision making.

However, the more significant innovation lies in strategic design. At Oxygen Conservation, projects combine rewilding with renewable energy, regenerative agriculture, and nature-based tourism. These layered revenue models resemble Software-as-a-Service (SaaS), but are grounded in ecological regeneration.

In 2024, Oxygen Conservation declined a £250 million investment because it would have constrained our operational agility. Just as early tech entrepreneurs resisted venture capital terms that compromised vision, nature innovators are protecting their mission to move fast, think differently, and stay purpose-driven.

Resilience as strategy: Nature and corporate risk management

Business resilience today demands integration with environmental systems. Climate instability is now a direct operational and financial risk. Companies that embed natural capital into their supply chains and risk frameworks are not just reducing harm, they are increasing adaptability.

Nature is the only infrastructure that strengthens over time. A restored watershed today offers long-term insurance (in every sense) against drought, water shortages, and wildfires. It also supports biodiversity and offers the potential for recreation and wellbeing. These outcomes are trackable and certifiable, giving business leaders measurable confidence.

Investing in ecosystems where unicorns roam

In 1994, backing the internet required foresight. Today, backing nature is almost embarrassingly obvious. The environmental crises we face demand investment strategies that are ethical, scalable, and profitable.

Nature has the potential to transform not only how we mitigate climate risk, but how we structure economies around resilience and regeneration. Nature is not the next Silicon Valley. It is something even bigger, and the green economic transition is already underway.

The next unicorns won't be digital avatars or yet another app. They'll be deeply rooted in real landscapes, scaling not through code alone, but through carbon, community, and climate resilience. The future economy will be regenerated by ecological intelligence, systems thinking, and radical collaboration.

Imagine the most exciting initial public offering (IPO) of the next decade: a company restoring thousands of acres of degraded land, issuing verified nature credits, generating wind energy, hosting ecotourism experiences, and using AI to monitor biodiversity gains in real time. This is where the smart money is moving, because ecosystems aren't mythical beasts. They're real, they're powerful, and they're where the next unicorns are already starting to roam.

The question for investors and business leaders won't be, 'Why support nature?' It will be, 'How did you miss the biggest green IPO of the century?'

On reflection

This was originally written for *The European Business Review*. Thank you so much for featuring our work and helping to widen the conversation around natural capital.

Unlocking Nature: Encouraging Public Access to Private Lands

Written November 2024

Picture this: a world where everyone, regardless of their background or circumstances, has the chance to roam freely across the stunning landscapes that our planet has to offer. This isn't just a utopian dream; it's a vision of an inclusive, environmentally conscious society.

From reducing stress and boosting mental health to fostering creativity and enhancing physical health, the benefits of spending time in nature are numerous and profound. Nature isn't just a backdrop for our lives; it's a crucial element of our wellbeing. Imagine the clarity of mind that comes from time spent in a temperate rainforest, the inspiration from watching a river carve its way through the landscape, or the sheer joy of breathing in the fresh, crisp air of the countryside. Every time we at Oxygen Conservation welcome visitors to our estates, we see the positive impact nature has on people.

To inspire a generation of environmental champions, we must ensure that people can experience and connect with nature first hand. It's hard to champion something you don't understand or value. By opening up our natural spaces, we create opportunities for people to build a personal connection with the environment. This connection fosters a deeper appreciation and a stronger commitment to protecting our planet.

The COVID-19 pandemic brought many challenges, but it also highlighted how much we value our natural spaces. When lockdowns restricted our movements, many of us longed for the simple pleasure of a walk in the park or a hike in the hills. This period underscored the importance of nature in our lives and made clear that access to these spaces is not just a luxury, but a necessity for our collective wellbeing.

In Scotland, the right to roam allows the public to access most land and inland water, providing a clear and straightforward framework for enjoying the natural world. This model simplifies the relationship between landowners and the public, promoting a culture of mutual respect and shared responsibility. Extending this right to England and Wales would in many ways simplify access and enhance the public's ability to enjoy and appreciate the environment, but even while championing public access, I am acutely aware of the difficulties.

The idea of open access is appealing, but the reality for landowners, especially those focused on conservation, is complex. The majority of people are courteous and respectful, but unfortunately, a significant (and impactful) minority are not. This minority can cause substantial damage, from littering and vandalism to more severe issues like fly-tipping, antisocial behaviour, and violence directed at people, property, and animals.

Let's delve into the realities of public access to land and explore the barriers.

The challenges faced by landowners

For farmers and landowners facing the combined impacts of climate change and economic pressures, along with all their other challenges, the idea of opening their land to the public can be daunting. The costs associated with repairing damage, managing access, and ensuring the safety of both visitors and the environment are significant.

It's incredibly important for people to recognise the risks that private landowners are exposed to without payment or mitigation as part of public access to their land. After all, it is in most cases *their* land. Would you be open to sharing your garden or maybe even your home with the public? It's essential to address these challenges to find a balanced approach, otherwise an increasing number of landowners will take matters into their own hands and say no, you're not welcome here.

Insights from the Earl of Devon

Charles Courtenay, the 19th Earl of Devon, shared his experiences on our podcast, highlighting the dual commitment to advocating for public access while managing the realities of land ownership. During his time at Powderham Castle, he has dealt with serious issues, including terrorism-related incidents, extensive fly-tipping, and even the brutal killing of livestock (a sheep bludgeoned to death with a baseball bat!). However, despite these experiences, he still advocates for public access while equally sharing the view that private landowners should be paid and protected when opening their land.

Balancing public access and environmental protection

As conservation-focused landowners, we at Oxygen Conservation face the paradox of encouraging public access while protecting the environment from potential harm. The inescapable fact is that people put pressure on the natural environment, and more people mean more pressure. Given the precarious state of nature in this country, we are at risk of loving parts of our natural environment to death.

This mirrors the challenges faced by national park CEOs, who must balance public enjoyment with conservation goals. Their jobs are almost impossible due to the conflicting demands of inviting more people into national parks while ensuring that these places and spaces are preserved and protected.

Managing risk and liability

Private landowners also face exposure to risk and liability that they haven't invited. At one of our estates in Scotland, the land is currently open to pedestrians and cyclists. Recently, there have been a small number of repeated requests from some parts of the community to open farming gates for vehicle access across the landscape. While this may seem a good way of encouraging wider community use, allowing vehicle traffic can create its own social and environmental challenges.

It presents health and safety risks, especially in remote areas due to unsuitable roads with significant drops on either side. It can lead to increases in noise and air pollution, which can harm sensitive habitats, and it can cause disruption and risk to people living on the land, particularly those with young children.

At another one of our estates, this time in Devon, we collaborated with the police to remove trespassers. A large group set up a permanent camp (advising our estate team that the camp would be increasing in size over the coming days), presenting a significant wildfire risk in the process. The cost (time and money) of dealing with such situations is substantial and impacts our ability to fund conservation initiatives effectively. I would like to note our thanks to the wonderful Devon and Cornwall Police for their fantastic support in resolving this matter.

Managing the health and safety aspect of public access can have an inhibitive impact on the types of conservation interventions that are undertaken. Public access can prevent owners from allowing herbivores to roam freely, leaving carcasses out to provide food for insects and scavengers, or creating space for water to spill naturally over the landscape in flood events. On top of this, it can place obligations on landowners that may run counter to the aims of conservation projects, from installing more built infrastructure into the environment, whether that be new fences, paths, or car parks, to cutting back trees and hedgerows rather than letting them grow naturally.

Encouraging private landowners to open more land

I always try to offer help or solutions where we find challenges. These ideas may give the government and local authorities food for thought:

- **Liability protection.** Oxygen Conservation would love to see the government implement policies that protect landowners from legal liabilities associated with public access. Clear guidelines and insurance options can provide peace of mind to those worried about potential legal issues.

- **Financial incentives.** Introduce government grants and subsidies for landowners who open their land to the public. This can help cover the costs of the maintenance, repairs, and infrastructure improvements needed to accommodate visitors.
- **Infrastructure support.** Provide support for building necessary infrastructure such as trails, signage, parking, and waste management facilities. Well-managed access points can reduce environmental impact and improve the visitor experience.
- **Community stewardship programmes.** Establish volunteer programmes where local communities help maintain and monitor public access areas. This can reduce the burden on landowners and foster a sense of shared responsibility and respect for the land.
- **Educational campaigns.** Launch campaigns to educate the public on responsible behaviour while accessing private land. Promoting awareness about the impact of littering, vandalism, and other negative behaviours helps mitigate these issues. This is something Camp Wild, which provides access to private land for environmentally conscious campers, has done incredibly well.
- **Partnerships with conservation organisations.** Encourage collaborations between landowners and conservation groups to create and manage public access areas. These groups can provide expertise, resources, and support to ensure sustainable and beneficial access.

- **Recognition and rewards.** Develop programmes that recognise and reward landowners for their contributions to public access and conservation. Awards, public acknowledgements, and certifications can enhance the reputation and morale of participating landowners.
- **Flexibility in access rights.** Allow landowners to designate specific areas for public access while protecting sensitive regions (assuming these are respected). This balance ensures that conservation efforts are not compromised while offering recreational opportunities.

A commitment to public access

Despite these challenges, we at Oxygen Conservation remain committed to finding ways to help people enjoy our estates sustainably. Initiatives like our ecotourism offer Oxygen Escapes, partnerships with Camp Wild, and plans to improve onsite facilities are steps towards providing better access. However, it's clear that we can't be everything to everyone, and some areas must remain restricted to protect sensitive ecosystems or those trying to recover from the impact of people in the past.

Public access to the natural world is a crucial aspect of fostering environmental stewardship and enhancing our collective wellbeing, but while the benefits are clear, the complexities and challenges faced by landowners must be acknowledged and addressed. Private landowners, especially those focused on conservation, often bear the brunt of issues such as littering, vandalism, and liability (at Oxygen Conservation, we've encountered them all and continue to do so). These challenges can make the idea of public access daunting and financially frightening.

To overcome these hurdles, we need a balanced and collaborative approach that encourages landowners to open their gates while providing them with the necessary support. Financial incentives, liability protections, community stewardship programmes, and educational campaigns are all essential tools in this effort. However, it is equally important that local communities play an active role in this partnership.

Communities can contribute by respecting the land, participating in volunteer stewardship programmes, and supporting landowners in maintaining and monitoring access areas. This collaborative spirit fosters a sense of shared responsibility and respect for the land, making public access a mutually beneficial endeavour. By offering their time, resources, and respect, communities help ensure that public access is sustainable and beneficial for everyone involved.

On reflection

Creating a future where the natural world is accessible to all requires thoughtful management, respectful engagement and innovative solutions. It also requires a strong partnership between landowners and communities. By working together, we can ensure that our natural spaces remain protected while being enjoyed by generations to come. Public access to private lands should not be seen as a demand, but as a collaborative effort where everyone has a role to play. Through this partnership, we can create a more inclusive, environmentally conscious society that values and protects the natural world.

No Farmers, No Food: A Dangerous Oversimplification

Written November 2024

One of the arguments we often hear (and see on billboards and road bridges) against land-use change is the wonderfully simple statement: 'No farmers, no food'. Its effectiveness lies in its absolute clarity. It's a bumper sticker slogan: easy to understand, catchy, and seemingly impossible to refute. But the truth is, simplicity tends to miss the point, and this is no exception.

I don't know a single person who believes we should have no farmers. Who are these imaginary enemies of farming? Who is making this absurd argument? 'No farmers, no food' is a straw man (something we need farmers for), designed to polarise debate and cause conflict. It's a slogan created to provoke, divide, and scare, rather than to inform or inspire meaningful conversation. It appeals to those who want things to be black and white, who reject the complexity, the nuance, and the difficult questions that we *should* be asking. The world is far too complex for anything but shades of grey now.

Let me be crystal clear: farmers are inextricable from, and, of course, absolutely essential to, our food security. A vast proportion of land in the UK should be, and is, used for farming. Estimates suggest around 70% is under agriculture, depending on which figures you choose to believe, but let's not argue about acres. We need food, and farmers grow food, and while I'm here, I strongly believe we should all be paying more for our food.

We need so much more than farmers

Here's where it gets uncomfortable. No farmers, no food fails to recognise that farmers are just one part of a much larger, more intricate web of dependencies. We need nature. We need birds, butterflies, and bees. No pollinators, no food.

Guess what: intensive farming practices are systematically destroying the habitats these creatures need to survive. In our rush to produce more and more, we're killing the very things that make food production possible. We need to be wasting less, using less, and producing less, not more.

Soil

Then there's soil. The six inches of earth that sits between us and total ecological collapse. No soil, no food, but each year, millions of tons of topsoil are washed into our rivers and seas, destroying habitats, polluting watercourses, and disappearing from our fields. While I'm here, no water, no food either.

Much of this erosion is a direct result of intensive farming, driven by a pursuit of short-term yields at the cost of long-term sustainability. The Oxygen Conservation team has literally visited a farm growing maize on a salt marsh! We're losing the ground beneath our feet, and no amount of rhetoric will replace it.

Energy

No energy, no food. Farming requires it, in abundance. The tractors, the combines, the processing plants, the transportation networks, all rely on energy, mostly from fossil fuels that are wreaking havoc on our climate, threatening the very seasons we rely on for successful harvests.

Instead, we need more clean energy, and this will mean land use change. Of course, we all know that we can't pursue renewable energy on high-quality farmland, so let's stop pretending we can. Without a stable climate, we can't grow food. It's that simple, yet we act as though the only thing threatening our food security is a supposed lack of farmers. The truth is, the entire system is under attack – from climate change, habitat destruction, soil degradation – and ignoring that reality won't make it go away.

No climate, no food.

High-quality farming

The harsh and blatantly obvious truth is this: our food system is broken.

Many farmers are responsible stewards of the land. At Oxygen Conservation, we see examples of this every day: farmers who are integrating wildlife conservation, soil health, and carbon sequestration into their operations. In fact, we work with some of the very best across our estates and beyond.

We should be celebrating and supporting these farmers by paying more for their food, shopping locally, buying organic, and acknowledging the true cost of production. We need to make it economically viable for farmers to farm in a way that doesn't destroy the future they're trying to secure, and not through subsidies. By their very nature, subsidies are intended to help stabilise a broken system.

Let's be honest about another uncomfortable truth: not all land should be farmed. Not all farming is good farming, and no, not all land should be grazed. At Oxygen Conservation, we do not target high-quality farmland; we recognise that Grade 1 and 2 arable land should be, and, of course, is, used for food production. Instead, we acquire land for conservation that should never have been farmed; land that was put into production only because of poorly thought-out subsidies that incentivised destruction rather than stewardship. This is land that, without extensive physical and chemical abuse, has little agricultural value, and even with those interventions, has failed to justify itself economically or ecologically. Otherwise, it wouldn't be for sale.

Therefore, while I agree that no farmers would mean no food, we need to ask ourselves tougher questions: what kind of farming do we actually need and what are we all willing to pay for? Do we want a food system that continues to obliterate habitats, degrade our soil, poison our water, and destroy wildlife, or do we want a system that supports farmers, feeds people, and restores the natural world?

'No farmers, no food' is a convenient slogan, but it's dangerously misleading. It suggests that we should carry on with business as usual, that farming as it exists today is sacrosanct and untouchable. The market is telling us something very different; perhaps we might like to listen. Business as usual is what got us here in the first place, a destination that no one is happy with – especially the farmers that the Oxygen Conservation team meets.

It's time we moved past the simplistic slogans and acknowledged the complex reality we face. We need farmers. We need soil. We need pollinators. We need clean energy. We need a stable climate. None of these exist in isolation and focusing on one while ignoring the others is a recipe for disaster.

Let's stop pretending it's simple and start having the real conversation. The one that recognises that our food system, like every other system we depend on, is interconnected, complex, and in desperate need of reform. Then we can work together to build something better.

On reflection

This piece was written before the uproar in 2025 from many in the farming community about changes to inheritance tax rules. For clarity, I'm not a fan of inheritance tax, I think it's morally wrong. I also believe the public sector is too large, taxes are too high, and the UK is becoming an increasingly difficult place to do business.

Just because someone grows food doesn't mean they should be exempt from the rules, yet some farmers have told the Oxygen Conservation team, time and again, that they believe the rules, any rules, shouldn't apply to them, because: 'No farmers, no food'. This comes across less like a fight for fairness and more like a demand for special treatment, regardless of the environmental or economic cost.

My view hasn't changed. Of course farmers are vital, but so are clean water, healthy soil, working ecosystems, and every other part of the system that gets food from field to plate. Food security doesn't rest on farmers alone. It relies on complexity and balance, but it's much simpler to just yell, 'No farmers, no food', isn't it?

How 'Just Planting More Trees' Could Be Bad for the Environment

Written November 2024

In recent years, it feels like almost everyone is yelling 'Let's just plant trees' as the answer to the environmental challenges we face, particularly in combating climate change and biodiversity loss. While this sentiment may be well-intentioned, the reality of woodland restoration is far more complex than simply putting any tree in any piece of ground. Without careful consideration of the ecological, social, and logistical aspects of such projects, tree planting can return diminished benefits or even be counterproductive.

At first glance, tree planting seems like a straightforward solution, and in an increasingly noisy world we are often drawn towards the apparently simple. Trees absorb carbon dioxide, provide habitats, and enhance the landscape. However, this logic oversimplifies the intricate dynamics at play in nature. There are numerous cases where poorly planned tree-planting initiatives have led to unintended consequences, such as disrupting local biodiversity, altering hydrological cycles, or even introducing invasive species that outcompete native flora. These issues highlight the importance of making informed choices when designing and executing woodland restoration projects.

A comprehensive approach considers far more than the number of trees planted. The choice of species, the origin and provenance of seed source, the condition of the soil, local climate factors, and the potential risks posed by invasive species or pathogens must be carefully evaluated. Oxygen Conservation's approach, for example, includes a focus on factors like biosecurity protocols, site-specific vegetation management, and long-term maintenance, which are all critical to ensuring successful, sustainable woodland restoration projects.

Why detail matters

Not all trees are created equally. Tree species selection is one of the most crucial elements of any restoration effort. Planting non-native species or those inappropriate for the local climate can create ecological imbalances, putting wildlife at risk. In some cases, fast-growing non-native species can deplete the soil of nutrients or alter water availability or movement, leading to broader environmental degradation.

For example, in regions where native oak or beech trees thrive, planting fast-growing species such as Sitka spruce or eucalyptus may seem beneficial in terms of carbon capture, but such species fail to support the rich biodiversity that native woodlands provide. They can also lower water tables or increase soil acidity, hindering the growth of other plants and disrupting existing ecosystems.

More than just dirt

Equally important is understanding the condition of the soil. Tree planting initiatives often neglect to consider healthy soil structure, microbial life, and the existing vegetation that may play a vital role in ecosystem stability. Soil compaction, poor drainage, and nutrient imbalances can all negatively impact the success of tree planting efforts. If we don't address these factors, newly planted trees may struggle to take root and thrive.

How we treat the ground is hugely important in woodland restoration projects. Minimal ground disturbance in preparation for planting is the best approach to avoid disrupting existing ecosystems. This approach leverages the natural advantages of the current plant community, such as moisture retention, temperature moderation, and the support of beneficial microorganisms.

Minimising plastic in the tree planting process

In our commitment to sustainability, we at Oxygen Conservation work incredibly hard to minimise the use of plastic throughout every stage of the tree planting process, whether it's in growing, delivery, or protection once planted. We strive to eliminate or drastically reduce single-use plastic by avoiding the use of tree guards, favouring reusable planting materials and plastic-free packaging for saplings. Additionally, we prioritise sourcing trees from nurseries that share our plastic-reduction ethos, ensuring that every step of the process reflects our broader commitment to ecological integrity and reducing our environmental footprint.

The spread of invasive species

In the globalised world, the risks of introducing invasive species and pathogens through tree planting activities are greater than ever. Many projects fail to consider the biosecurity risks posed by non-native pathogens or organisms that may be introduced with imported saplings. The devastating effects of diseases such as ash dieback or Phytophthora root rot, which have wiped out vast areas of woodland across Europe, should serve as a stark reminder that tree planting is not without its environmental risks.

At Oxygen Conservation, we apply biosecurity measures in every project to protect against these risks. This includes sourcing trees from certified nurseries (all of which we visit ahead of time) and maintaining meticulous records of tree health and origin. It also involves inspecting saplings for diseases, ensuring that equipment used on multiple sites is thoroughly cleaned, and making use of disinfectant protocols where necessary.

Partnerships make perfect

Partnering with expert advisors and specialists like TreeStory is essential for the success of woodland restoration projects. Their in-depth knowledge of ecosystems, species selection, and land management ensures that restoration efforts are tailored to the specific needs of each landscape. By working with specialists, we can achieve more resilient and sustainable outcomes that benefit both the environment and local communities.

It's about the long term

A critical aspect often overlooked in tree planting projects is the long-term maintenance of newly restored woodlands. Trees require care and monitoring in their early years to ensure survival. This might include watering, mulching, weeding, or replacing saplings that fail to thrive, or even survive. The establishment phase is when trees are at their most vulnerable, and without a clear post-planting care strategy, the initial effort and significant investment can be lost.

Incorporating local communities where possible (and where they are willing) in the ongoing care and management of woodland areas not only helps reduce costs, but fosters a sense of ownership and stewardship over these spaces. This social dimension is essential to the initiation and long-term success of any ecological project. Collaborative initiatives with community engagement, such as volunteer programmes, educational workshops, and the use of local knowledge, can ensure that the restored woodland continues to benefit both people and wildlife for generations to come.

Thoughtful woodland restoration

Tree planting is a wonderful thing when done thoughtfully with a deep understanding of the local ecology and a commitment to long-term care, but alone it's not a silver bullet for climate change or biodiversity loss. Instead, it must be part of a broader, more holistic strategy for landscape restoration. This includes protecting existing forests, restoring degraded lands, and enhancing natural processes such as rewilding, landscape connectivity, and flood management.

Tree planting can play a critical role in this, but we must shift the narrative from 'just plant trees' to 'plant the right trees in the right place, for the right reasons, at the right time'. Only then will our efforts contribute meaningfully to restoring ecosystems, enhancing biodiversity, and mitigating climate change.

On reflection

This is a reflection on a recent trip to Esgair Arth, Oxygen Conservation's beautiful estate in West Wales, where we've spent the last two years meticulously planting trees and encouraging spectacular natural regeneration.

It began, as many journeys in Wales do, on miles of waterlogged roads. It was the kind of day that only turns grey when the morning light finally breaks through the continuous rain. As we crested the hill leading down into Cardigan Bay, the rain paused just long enough to unveil the familiar expanse of sea, shimmering for what looked like forever. No matter how many times we see it, that view never loses its magic. It was one of those many moments that remind me how lucky I am to do this very thing at this very time.

We'd been battling the weather for days, but for once, the forecast got it wrong. Wales surprised us with a perfectly timed respite. That said, the aftermath of the storms was everywhere: roads veined with floodwater, fields transformed into sodden marshes, and ditches running wild. Despite the chaos, the landscape retained a certain type of rugged beauty: a working countryside of sheep-dotted hillsides and industrial farms.

As we neared Esgair Arth, the scene changed. Here, on the edge of Cardigan Bay, nature is writing a new story. The estate feels wet, wild, and wonderfully untamed. A messiness that signals life reclaiming its place. Esgair Arth is not just a landscape; it's a living, breathing example of landscape-scale restoration.

Years of industrial land use had left their marks: fences that suffocated natural movement, invasive species that crowded out native growth, and a sense of ecological imbalance. Today, those scars are healing, and quickly. We've removed kilometres of fencing, releasing the ancient site of special scientific interest (SSSI) woodland from its shackles. Lichen-draped branches rise from the Arth Valley like characters from a Tolkien novel, their earthly forms embodying a mythical beauty, almost scrambling up the hillside now they're once again free.

Thanks to the relentless work of our estate manager and a dedicated community of volunteers, much of the invasive vegetation has been removed, creating space for naturally regenerating native species. There is still work to do with plans for the felling of dominant beech trees crafted in consultation with the incredible environmental experts that call this part of Wales home, but this is not just restoration; it's a partnership, a collaboration between local knowledge and ecological ambition.

This model demonstrates the heart of what we do. We're constantly navigating the balance: creating green careers while fostering volunteer opportunities that connect people to the landscapes they call home. Here at Esgair Arth, we're finding that sweet spot where wildlife, people, and purpose converge, and I'm so proud for the team that they can craft and share the stories of their part of Wales.

Walking the former fence lines, we hear tales of newly discovered wild service trees: the northernmost examples of this rare species in the UK. The landscape, once silent and abused, hums with life. Field voles dart underfoot, while owls swoop low in the early morning light, gliding on silent wings in search of the now plentiful breakfast. The abundance isn't just noticeable; it's tangible. This is what regeneration looks like, not in theory, but in movement, sound, temperature, texture, and vitality.

Esgair Arth is a study in contrasts. On one side of the estate, huge amounts of fencing have been removed to let nature take the lead. Here, the SSSI woodland thrives through natural regeneration, each seed and sprout part of a wild, unplanned masterpiece. On the other side, the approach is different. With little natural seed stock and decades of agricultural impact, including pesticides, fertilisers, and almost constant compaction, the landscape needed a little more help. More than 100,000 trees have been planted by specialist contractors, each one a promise of a future forest. The brilliant team at Delta Forest has been crucial here, blending precision and passion to professionalise the tree-planting sector – we need more innovative startups like this, we need an entire ecosystem.

This duality, letting nature lead in some areas while providing a helping hand in others, defines our work. It's a testament to the flexibility required to Scale Conservation. Each tool, whether it's a spade, a chainsaw, or just plentiful patience, plays a role in the symphony of restoration.

There's something profoundly grounding about time spent in landscapes like this. On this wild Welsh day, as the rain comes and goes in unpredictable bursts, I'm overcome with gratitude for the team, for the land, and for the privilege of being part of something so transformative. The work at Esgair Arth is a living, breathing testament to our purpose: creating spaces where people and wildlife not only coexist, but truly belong, side by side.

This is the messy, magical soul of conservation. It's rarely elegant, never easy, and often unpredictable, but it is always worth it. Through the rain and the mud, through quiet victories and loud, unruly challenges, we are building something enduring; something that connects the past, present, and future in ways only nature can.

As we leave Esgair Arth, the lichen-clad branches stand like ancient sentinels, their forms swaying gently in the wind. It feels as though they're raising a quiet farewell whispering, 'Thank you and until next time', and then I realise that those words are actually mine.

The Ground-Nesting Bird Excuse

Written January 2025

One of the recurring lines we hear in relation to land management is 'What about ground-nesting birds?' It's a question often used to justify practices that cause devastating environmental damage, whether they're the killing of 'predators' like foxes, burning the hillsides, or discouraging woodland restoration. The argument is that these practices are necessary to produce optimum conditions for these species, but we have to ask ourselves, why have ground-nesting birds become the single metric of environmental success?

One of my rules in life is to listen to understand, not just to respond. This question has permeated conversations with land managers, farmers, naturalists, and even sporting enthusiasts. Without fail, the rationale for it is deeply intertwined with tradition, particularly grouse shooting. While many of those involved in the sport recognise that reshaping entire landscapes just to create conditions that might produce more of the one thing they aim to shoot is fundamentally flawed, ground-nesting birds offer a moral smokescreen (irony fully intended if anyone has seen the abomination that is muirburn). If it's claimed that it's all 'for the good of ground-nesting birds', it feels more acceptable. We go from being vandals to custodians of nature. It's easier to own the destruction of wildlife and habitat if it's framed as something virtuous, isn't it?

In truth, what we've done is develop overwrought narratives and dissociative language to help people feel comfortable with the damage inflicted on the landscape; it's everywhere in the land economy. It's a way to reconcile the obsession with controlling nature and the paradoxical desire to protect it (in the form we want), when really, it's about the desire to kill something, whether for sport or out of an illusion of management.

Where ground-nesting birds really flourish

Let's pause to remember where ground-nesting birds originally thrived, long before we manipulated their habitats for our purposes. Across Europe, these species flourished in vast floodplains, open glades, and naturally occurring clearings. For example, curlews in Finland are often found nesting amongst bog pines, bracken, wooded landscapes – natural mosaics that offer protection and resources. Closer to home, snipe in Rothiemurchus call from the tops of trees in dynamic landscapes shaped by wetlands and woodlands. These birds did not evolve in scorched predator-free monoculture moorlands, but in rich, diverse environments shaped by natural forces like flooding, forest dynamics, and grazing from native herbivores.

What if we shifted our focus? Instead of manipulating the environment to create ideal conditions for the one species we want to kill, we could reduce human intervention and allow nature to take the lead. Floodplains could be restored, creating vast biodiverse wetlands. Woodland glades and clearings, which once offered ideal habitats for these birds, could naturally reappear as forests are allowed to regenerate.

These are the kinds of landscapes where ground-nesting birds thrive.

Let nature lead the way

Imagine a landscape free from chemical inputs, where burning wasn't used as a tool of control, and the invasive species humans introduced were actively removed to allow ecosystems to self-correct. Rather than imposing our will, we could let nature find its own equilibrium, one that is responsive to climate changes, biodiversity, and natural cycles, not human timetables, sporting calendars, or fiscal years.

In such a system, we wouldn't need to obsess over whether or not ground-nesting birds are thriving at any given moment; everything would be better as a result. Biodiversity would ebb and flow as ecosystems evolved, supporting a wider range of species and creating conditions far richer and more dynamic than any artificially maintained landscape. Ground-nesting birds, along with countless other species, could flourish in an environment where natural processes determined the health of the land, not the interventionist hand of managers and gamekeepers.

The language of arrogance, dominance, and destruction is literally hiding in plain sight. Our current model, driven by the need to control (which often means to kill), only serves to diminish the resilience and richness of our ecosystems, ironically resulting in far fewer of the very things the most passionate proponents for tradition want to see. Virtually every traditional gamekeeper we meet reflects that 'numbers are down', with most concluding that they will keep doing what they're doing, or worse, push harder.

It's time to step back and give nature the chance to heal, to thrive, and to exist on *its* terms, not ours. Only then can we hope to create a truly healthy, abundant environment that serves all forms of life, not just the ones we've decided matter most.

On reflection

Revisiting this piece, I feel even more strongly that we've tolerated a dangerous, manipulative narrative for too long, one that insists we need to dominate, control, and often kill nature to care for it. The ground-nesting bird excuse has become a tired, overplayed refrain from those desperate to justify scorched landscapes and dead foxes as acts of stewardship, but make no mistake, we don't need to kill something to protect or enjoy the environment.

Yes, ground-nesting birds matter. Of course they do, but they don't matter more than everything else. They don't justify torching the land. They don't excuse systematic predator extermination. They definitely don't give us a moral free pass because we like shooting the very things we claim to be saving. What is the acceptable exchange of death to allow us to kill another brace of grouse?

We need to stop pretending this is about protection. It's about power. It's about control. In too many cases, it's about ego, arrogance, and what has always been done.

What's most revealing is that even the people clinging to these traditions admit it's not working. 'Numbers are down,' they say, but instead of changing course, they double down. More killing. More burning. More intervention. When will we acknowledge that this obsession with management isn't a solution, it's the problem?

We've lost sight of something crucial: nature doesn't need us to control it to thrive. In fact, it thrives in our absence. Ground-nesting birds evolved in dynamic, complex landscapes: floodplains, wetlands, broken woodlands – places shaped by water, weather, and wildness. Not sterile scorched moors. Not monocultures engineered to maximise shooting days.

If our version of conservation demands blood, fire, and the illusion of control, then let's call it what it is: a horrific performance. A curated wilderness, managed like a museum exhibit; taxidermied landscapes dressed in tradition, preserved for ego, not ecology.

At Oxygen Conservation, when we intervene, we do so reluctantly, with reverence and respect, and only because the balance has already been broken.

Transparency Paradox

Written August 2024

Increasingly, everyone talks about wanting transparency, especially in the environmental sector, where criticism and suspicion of greenwashing run high. However, people often realise that ignorance is bliss when reality forces them to confront the consequences of transparency. In conservation, decisions are rarely black and white, and rarer yet always green. The moment we pull back the curtain on the realities of land management, we uncover a world of complexities, compromises, and difficult choices that many would rather not acknowledge.

Land management is incredibly complicated, and modernising a sector steeped in tradition, pride, anger, resentment, and polarising views is an immense challenge. I've written extensively about how Oxygen Conservation encounters contradictions and compromises on a daily basis, rarely having the opportunity to take the perfect course of action. Instead, we must balance a wide range of competing social, environmental, technological, political, ideological, and economic priorities.

It's easy to criticise a course of action when we don't have to suggest an alternative or engage with the realities of the world as it is, not as we wish it to be. Oxygen Conservation encountered a real example of this challenge at our estate in the Scottish Borders, where we made the difficult decision to cull a large number of wild goats due to their rapid population increase and severe impact on the environment.

A landscape in crisis

When we acquired the estate, we inherited a landscape devoid of trees, with biodiversity almost totally absent. It is desperately in need of restoration and recovery, but not everyone shares this perspective. For some who have known this place for years, it is beautiful just as it is, and the idea of change, even environmental restoration, is offensive.

One of the most prominent requests we heard from more than fifty members of the local community when we first acquired the estate was for transparency about our actions. On that basis, we committed to sharing what we were planning to do and why.

On acquiring the estate, we inherited a population of wild goats, fascinating creatures with almost warrior-like colours and distinctly medieval horns. These goats are non-native and unprotected. Without accurate numbers, as is so often the case across large landscapes, we conducted thermal drone surveys to track their population numbers. Over twelve months, we saw their numbers grow significantly, from around 20 to more than 130.

The impact of excessive grazing, well-documented in reference to sheep and deer across the UK, especially in Scotland, is devastating. It completely halts natural woodland regeneration, damages peatland, and devastates flora and biodiversity.

Government policy has continued to veer away from installing additional fencing, preferring to reduce animal numbers instead. This shift is largely influenced by public access concerns and, perhaps ironically, community pressure to maintain open landscapes. Fencing can (in the absence of gates) restrict recreational access and create tensions with local communities. There are also concerns that fencing can disrupt wildlife corridors, hinder broader conservation efforts, and lead to unintended ecological consequences, making animal population control a more politically popular approach, until it isn't. We have sympathies for both perspectives, there is never a single right answer everywhere, demonstrating why the role of government is impossible.

The tendency to prioritise the less unpopular approach over the more complex course of action has led to the phrase 'bullets over fencing' being openly discussed by government officials. However, this approach is not without its critics or obvious consequences.

The hypocrisy of criticism

It's interesting to consider what is 'normal' for a traditional estate. Across the UK, many estates are involved in agriculture, breeding and slaughtering cattle, sheep, pigs, and poultry. Many stock pheasants and partridges for shooting, or optimise landscapes for game birds (largely grouse), while killing crows, foxes, stoats, and weasels to name but a few of the so-called 'predators'. Some sporting estates have even been associated with the illegal killing of protected raptors to preserve game bird populations.

At Oxygen Conservation, we do not stock or shoot birds. We have removed sheep farming from our estates. We do not allow trapping of crows, nor of weasels, stoats, or other mustelids. We are even challenging regulatory pressure to cull fox numbers where no data supports such actions.

We do not want to kill anything, but sometimes, conservation requires difficult choices. We explored multiple alternatives, including relocation, but these either were logistically unfeasible (or simply not allowed) due to the difficulty of capturing and safely transporting wild goats, which posed risks to the goats themselves, or would have resulted in further ecological damage by shifting the problem elsewhere rather than addressing it at the source. We therefore, reluctantly, reduced the population through humane culling, ensuring the long-term restoration of the landscape.

Transparency – the double-edged sword

When we acquire land, local communities want to know what we are doing and why, even before we have the opportunity to listen to and learn from the landscape itself. We believe in a transparent approach – honest, open, and evidence-based – but the incident described above highlights a paradox: many people believe they want transparency until they are faced with the reality it reveals.

For every hostile email we received, there were quiet acknowledgments from local landowners and stakeholders, people who supported our approach but feared public backlash if they spoke up. They referred to significant ecological damage on other estates, along with health and safety threats posed by the increasing number of goats on public roads across the area.

Our experience in Scotland underscores why so few landowners actually engage openly with the public on difficult decisions. If they do, they are open to being criticised and attacked.

Is this really the way we want land management to work in future?

Why we will keep being honest

Why doesn't Oxygen Conservation take the easier route and keep these decisions in the shadows? There are members of our team who make this exact challenge, especially the ones that are threatened, insulted, or abused as a result of transparency.

The answer is because being honest is the right thing to do. Because ignorance has led humans to consume unsustainably, avoid difficult conversations, and choose easy outrage over engaged understanding, discussion, debate, and innovative solutions.

Conservation is nuanced, full of tough choices and imperfect solutions. At Oxygen Conservation, every decision we make is informed by data, carefully considered, and responsibly delivered. It includes independent expert surveys, advice, and guidance, alongside ongoing community engagement. No, that doesn't mean everyone who has an opinion, because that's just not possible, and not every opinion is created equally. We will continue doing the right thing for people and wildlife, even when these choices are hard – confident in the knowledge that it is literally impossible to please everyone.

Which would you choose, transparency or blissful ignorance?

On reflection

The lesson here is about courage. About what happens when you lift the veil and show the reality of land management: not the curated countryside some wish for, but the messy, complex, difficult business of making ecological decisions in a broken system.

We were told to be transparent, so we were. We shared the data, the rationale, the context. We engaged early. We listened, and we still got shouted at, sometimes by people who hadn't read a word of the explanation, sometimes by people who didn't know anything about the land in question.

That's the paradox. People demand openness, but when you give it to them raw – especially when it challenges their assumptions, they recoil. They don't want *transparency*, they want *reassurance*, and that's not the same thing.

What I've learned is that real transparency isn't just hard to deliver, it's often punished. I also know this: without it, trust dies. Accountability fades. Conservation becomes a closed room where nothing new can happen and no one learns.

We'll keep choosing sunlight over shadows, even when it burns, because if we're not willing to be honest, then we have no business asking others to change. The alternative is easy: keep secrets, make decisions behind closed doors, and let the system carry on as it has, quietly failing. That's not leadership, and it's not good enough.

Here's the question we all need to ask ourselves, landowners, policymakers, communities, campaigners alike: do we want to *feel* good or do we want to *do* good? Because sometimes – actually most of the time – we don't get both.

We're Living in the Renaissance for Natural Capital Innovation

Written September 2025

We are currently experiencing a pivotal transformation in how natural capital is perceived and integrated into society. No longer a peripheral concern, natural capital has emerged at the forefront of business strategy, financial planning, public policy, and cultural expression. This shift mirrors the historic Renaissance: a time of reimagining systems, challenging conventions, and pioneering new paradigms.

The urgency of environmental degradation and climate instability has galvanised innovation across multiple domains. What makes this moment exceptional is the diversity and speed of the response: vibrant, experimental, and brimming with possibility. The natural world is no longer an afterthought in strategic decision making. It is a primary focus, rightly influencing how organisations operate, allocate resources, and envision their future. This is a systemic transformation, guided by a fundamental reconsideration of value.

Cross-sector collaboration

An unprecedented convergence is occurring across industries:

- Financial institutions are mobilising billions in climate and biodiversity funds, from private investment to sovereign wealth vehicles and rewilding bonds. These instruments are actively shaping the flow of capital towards projects that generate ecological, social, and financial returns.
- Technologists are deploying AI, LiDAR, satellite imagery, and environmental DNA (eDNA) to quantify and monitor ecological variables at unprecedented resolution. Data-driven insights are enabling smarter, faster, and more transparent environmental decision making.
- Cultural creators are reshaping narratives around land use and ecological value through platforms like TikTok, YouTube, and podcasts. They are turning ecological insight into everyday content, shifting public perception in real time and helping more people reconnect with the natural world.
- Agricultural stakeholders are transitioning from conventional to regenerative practices, embedding organic and ecological thinking into daily operations. These practices not only restore soil and ecosystems, but also provide new avenues for revenue and resilience.

This convergence is accelerating talent into the natural capital economy. High-calibre professionals from sectors like Big Tech and finance are joining the movement, evidencing a fundamental shift in career aspirations and priorities.

This is especially apparent amongst the most talented young people, whose extraordinary capabilities and fresh perspectives are energising the sector in ways previously unimaginable, and whose talents the environmental field could not have attracted until now. Their influence is reshaping what it means to be a conservationist, pushing the field towards greater interdisciplinarity, purpose, and ambition.

Reimagining systems and methodologies

This era is not merely about reforming outdated structures; it is about constructing entirely new ones that align economic systems with ecological principles, integrating resilience, adaptability, and community engagement at every level:

- **Technological innovation.** Measurement, reporting, and verification (MRV) systems are being revolutionised through the application of cutting-edge tools such as AI, eDNA, remote sensing, and blockchain technologies. These systems provide higher-resolution data, enable real-time monitoring, and foster transparency in how ecosystem services are quantified and traded.
- **Business innovation.** Revenue models are shifting towards a diversified stack of ecosystem service streams, including carbon sequestration, biodiversity uplift, nutrient neutrality, and watershed management. This evolution supports the rise of vertically integrated land-based enterprises that are

simultaneously ecological stewards and commercial operators, breaking the old binary between conservation and profit.

- **Regulatory and procedural frameworks.** Novel standards like the UK's BNG, voluntary carbon offset codes, and emerging ecosystem service protocols are redefining the rulebook for environmental governance. They are also pushing the frontier in community participation and equitable benefit sharing, catalysing trust and legitimacy.

These innovations are not simply technological advancements; they represent a paradigm shift in what it means to be effective in conservation. Success now requires fluency across ecology, data science, economics, law, and ethics and the ability to integrate these domains in real-world projects. The speed and depth of this transformation are especially evident in how quickly educational institutions, investors, and practitioners are adapting to this new interdisciplinary reality. Universities are launching new programmes, start-ups are accelerating their product development, and global standards are being rethought in response to this groundswell of innovation.

Cultural transformation in conservation

The evolution isn't just technical, it's cultural:

- The mindset is moving from ownership to stewardship, from extraction to regeneration. It's a philosophical shift with practical consequences, altering how individuals, communities, and corporations interact with the land.

- Communication strategies are democratising knowledge through storytelling, social media, and immersive experiences. Conservationists are becoming content creators, using new tools to reach diverse audiences and drive behavioural change.
- Ecotourism is transforming into a vehicle for engagement and education, integrating ecological literacy and leisure. Rewilding safaris, bioacoustics trails, and hands-on habitat restoration are connecting people to nature in unforgettable, visceral ways.

Culture is not lagging behind the environmental movement; it is helping drive it forward. The stories we tell about land, nature, and our responsibilities are shifting. This change in narrative is essential to building the collective will to support systemic reform.

Talent and capital: Engines of transformation

Talent development

The demand for skilled professionals in conservation finance, ecological operations, and stakeholder engagement is surging. Oxygen Conservation is pioneering an academy model to attract and develop high-potential talent. A cornerstone of this is our intern programme, which offers immersive hands-on experiences across the business, in areas including ecological operations, carbon project development, regenerative agriculture, and natural capital finance.

We deliberately recruit exceptional individuals, often people early in their careers or making bold pivots, who bring fresh energy, intellectual curiosity, and a deep commitment to positive change. Interns work directly alongside our leadership team, gaining exposure to strategic decision making and contributing meaningfully to our live projects.

This programme is not just a stepping stone; it's a talent pipeline, equipping future leaders with the interdisciplinary skills needed to thrive in the natural capital sector. It blends theory with practice, fostering individuals who can operate at the complex intersection of land, capital, and community.

Capital mobilisation

Investment is scaling rapidly, supported by:

- The evolution of philanthropic capital – no longer confined to traditional grants, it is increasingly being deployed as catalytic capital that seeks modest mission-aligned returns or operates under perpetual gifting models.
- Genuine private investment accelerating the sector's development – driving innovation and delivering risk-adjusted returns that align financial interests with ecological integrity.
- Private equity funds integrating long-term sustainability metrics, such as carbon risk, biodiversity impact, and social benefit outcomes, into their investment theses – signalling a broader shift in the market's understanding of what constitutes value.
- Institutional funds creating dedicated allocations to natural capital investments, often as part of their impact or ESG mandates. These allocations include diversified portfolios across carbon credits,

regenerative agriculture, water management, and habitat restoration, reflecting both a strategic imperative and a recognition of growing market demand for credible nature-based assets.

The capital flows are real, but the systems for their ethical deployment are still emerging, and that fluidity is where opportunity lives. As market norms are established, now is the time to shape capital pathways to prioritise integrity, equity, and impact over short-term gain. Aligning capital with meaningful ecological outcomes requires intentionality, rigorous standards, and continuous evaluation.

This window of innovation is finite

Like all developing sectors, the natural capital sector will mature, and faster than we may think. The evolution towards consolidation and standardisation is both inevitable and necessary for long-term stability. However, it also means the current phase of rapid experimentation and flexible frameworks will not last indefinitely.

Based on past experience, this is what I predict will happen:

- Standards will formalise, potentially locking in early decisions that may be difficult to reverse later.
- Institutional actors will become dominant, shaping norms, funding flows and strategic priorities.
- Regulatory regimes will tighten, reducing flexibility but offering greater accountability and trust.
- Innovation, while still present, will stabilise into established best practices that may limit radical creativity.

We are standing at a crossroads. This moment, chaotic, generative, experimental, is precious precisely because it is impermanent. What we choose to build and endorse now will define the boundaries and possibilities of the sector in the decades ahead. The freedom to explore unorthodox methods, challenge traditional models, and co-create new frameworks is a luxury of this brief window. Today's brave decisions, whether about ownership models, pricing strategies, or stakeholder inclusion, will become tomorrow's industry norms, frameworks, and expectations.

This is our opportunity to encode integrity, inclusivity, and innovation at the root of the system. Once they begin to ossify, it becomes exponentially harder to rewrite the rules.

Defining the next decades

The foundational questions that we must grapple with are not only technical but deeply philosophical. They strike at the heart of how we relate to nature, to one another, and to future generations:

- Who do we empower and elevate as thought leaders, storytellers, and stewards of this sector?
- What metrics will define success: short-term outputs or long-term systemic regeneration?
- How do we fairly balance ecological imperatives with financial viability, without commodifying nature in destructive ways?
- Who gains access to land, data, markets, and decision making, and who is excluded by default?

These questions are urgent, and they demand answers rooted in fairness, humility, and critical thought. We must be intentional, courageous, and willing to interrogate our own assumptions. The structures we set up now – governance, finance, legal rights, benefit-sharing – will determine whether this Renaissance becomes a true reformation or just another fleeting well-meaning trend that lost its edge when the stakes got real.

We are laying the foundations of a new sector. It must be built to last, but also evolve. Let's ensure that it is resilient, inclusive, and transformative from the very start. Above all, let's enjoy it. This period of energy, creativity, and collaborative spirit is rare. It's precious to be part of something bigger than ourselves, so let's be fully present in it, celebrate its messiness, and make the most of the magic while it lasts.

On reflection

One of my favourite reminders in life is that this too will pass. Moments like this, when the world feels alive with possibility and the pace of change is electric, are painfully temporary. They never announce their arrival, they never linger as long as we hope, and they're gone before we know it.

We're standing inside a rare pocket of creative chaos where ideas collide, disciplines blend, and the rules haven't been written yet. It's the kind of moment that only makes sense in hindsight, when people look back (perhaps in a book) and say they wish they'd realised what they were part of before it was too late.

I'm trying to realise it now, because this is the messy, brilliant, uncomfortable, unpredictable phase that future leaders will envy. The sector will mature. The edges will sharpen. The freedom will disappear. That's the cycle, but right here, right now, we get to experiment, to push boundaries, to be unreasonably ambitious, and to build a system that reflects integrity rather than apologises for its absence.

Maybe that's the real challenge: to enjoy this golden age even as we work to bring about its end.

This too will pass, although I wish it wouldn't!

Conclusion

There's a certain kind of leader. One who knows their people so well they can read the hesitation in an email, the tiredness in a voice, the concern in a silence. One who carries their team like family, even when they pretend it isn't so. One who loves what they do so deeply it scares people, and sometimes even scares them.

If that's you, then I see you. I know what it takes. I know what you give. I know the way you fill the gaps so no one else falls through. I know the cost of being the person everyone turns to. I know how often you find yourself coming second, or third, or fourth, or nowhere at all.

You don't get to choose when to lead. You don't get to switch off. Even when you tell yourself you could say no, the truth is you can't. Not really. Not when someone you care about needs you. Not when the mission is burning, bright and fragile at the same time. Not when you've built something that feels too important to leave unattended.

I know what it feels like when it's late and dark and you're far from home. When the hotel room is too hot or too cold (sometimes both at the same time) and your bag still isn't unpacked. When your children grow a little older each time you refresh the photo on your phone. When your own bed feels familiar, but at the same time like a holiday because you're so rarely there. When everyone thinks you're succeeding. When they tell you they want the view, but you know they don't want the climb.

You're an addict. Not in the way people whisper about; in the way society applauds. Addicted to purpose. Addicted to the rush of solving problems no one else can carry. Addicted to the rare feeling of being absolutely necessary. Addicted to building something bigger than you. Addicted to this.

You want more. More moments where your vision and your team feel like they're moving in the same direction. You want to feel alive, and sometimes you wish you didn't need it as much as you do.

I see the nights when you keep going long after everyone else has gone to sleep. The mornings when you don't remember what day it is. When you work through the discomfort. Through the pain. Through the tiredness. Through the impossible expectations you claim don't affect you. Through the pressure, all the pressure.

You can't miss that meeting. You can't delegate that opportunity. You can't drop that ball because someone else might break if you do. Sometimes you have to lead. Sometimes it has to be you. Sometimes you hate that truth. Sometimes you love it more than you should.

I know all of this for one simple reason: I'm you.

I know the burden and the privilege. The exhaustion and the euphoria. The weight of building a business that can change the world. The price of caring. The strange and stubborn joy of leading people you adore. The ache of wanting to give them everything and somehow finding a little more each time you think you can't.

This is the path we chose. Maybe it's the path that chose us. Either way, here we are. Still standing. Still trying. Still believing. Still caring too much. Still carrying more than anyone knows. Still telling ourselves tomorrow we might rest. Still knowing we won't.

To you: the founder, the scaling CEO, the leader who refuses to stop loving your people, I see you. I'm with you. You're not alone in this.

Ecosystem Alpha awaits

If there's one thing I've learned since Oxygen Conservation started, it's this: the rules are being rewritten faster than most people realise. By the time you've finished reading this book, we'll be onto something else entirely.

That's the nature of transformation. It doesn't move in neat chapters. Just like an upland gravel-bed river system, it loops and twists and accelerates, especially when we're operating at the messy intersection of conservation, capital, and culture.

This book began as a collection of essays, a snapshot of our thinking, our learning, and our doing – but in writing it, I've come to see it as something else: a record of a sector in metamorphosis. Not a tidy origin story or a polished case study, but a living, breathing account of what it feels like to build something real in real time. One estate, one river, one tree, one wild idea at a time.

At Oxygen Conservation, we've made mistakes. We've been challenged, doubted, and, yes, criticised. We've also seen extraordinary progress: thousands of acres being restored, species returned, water systems reconnected, jobs created, communities engaged (and outraged), and a market beginning to emerge that will one day support all of this at scale.

We're not volunteers. We're professionals. We're systems builders. We're disrupters. We're not here to conserve what was, we're here to reimagine what could be and make that a reality.

Now the next move comes into view. Everything we've done so far hasn't just been about Scaling Conservation. It was about preparing for the next chapter of Oxygen Conservation: Ecosystem Alpha. You might think the name hints at something financial, an upstart hedge fund with billions of capital ready to deploy. That's no accident. It's very much our intent.

We're taking the logic of natural capital, the deep value embedded in biodiversity, carbon, water, and soil, and using it to rewire financial markets. Not by pitching nature as a charity case, but by proving, unequivocally, that nature is *alpha*. That it can perform over the long term. That it can deliver returns – resilient, regenerative, and radically aligned with life itself.

That's where we're going. Together. Environment. Impact. Adventure. In equal measure.

Adventure is what this has always been. Not the kind of adventure you find talked about in boardrooms or branding decks. The real kind. The kind where you mountain bike down dry riverbeds, negotiate nature credits while knee deep in mud, open up lands that haven't welcomed the public in generations, and then try to explain it all on a podcast between gun shots echoing from a nearby estate. The kind of adventure that tests your convictions. Pushes you way beyond your comfort zone. Forces you to learn fast, and then asks you to do it again tomorrow.

Ecosystem Alpha isn't just a business model. It's a mindset. One built on curiosity, courage, and the willingness to act in uncertainty. One that knows the best ideas usually start as things people laugh at, or ignore, or dismiss as impossible. We've learned to take that as encouragement.

If you've made it this far, through the cricket analogies and carbon credit complexities, through reflections and rants and river rewigglings, I want to say thank you. Thank you for taking the time to read. To think. To challenge and question and imagine. Because if we're going to Scale Conservation, professionalise the sector, and unlock nature as an asset class, we'll need more people like you, curious, committed, and crazy enough to do things differently.

We're building this in real time. That means there's still space to shape it.

Over to you…

Bibliography

Books

DiPerna, P, *Pricing the Priceless: The financial transformation to value the planet, solve the climate crisis, and protect our most precious assets* (Wiley, 2023)

Dukes, A, *Thinking in Bets: Making smarter decisions when you don't have all the facts* (Portfolio Penguin, 2018)

Guidara, W, *Unreasonable Hospitality: The remarkable power of giving people more than they expect* (Portfolio, 2022)

Hannigan, R, *Counter-Intelligence: What the secret world can teach us about problem solving and creativity* (HarperCollins, 2024)

Lewis, M, *Moneyball: The art of winning an unfair game* (WW Norton & Company, 2004)

Maples, M; Ziebelman, P, *Pattern Breakers: Why some start-ups change the future* (PublicAffairs, 2024)

Scott, K, *Radical Candor: How to get what you want by saying what you mean* (Macmillan, 2017)

Sutherland, R, *Alchemy: The dark art and curious science of creating magic in brands, business, and life* (Collins, 2021)

Syed, M, *Black Box Thinking: Growth mindset and the secrets of high performance* (John Murray, 2025)

Szymanski, S; Wigmore, T, *Crickonomics: The anatomy of modern cricket* (Bloomsbury Sport, 2023)

Thiel, P; Masters, B, *Zero to One: Notes on start-ups, or how to build the future* (Virgin Books, 2015)
Welchman, G, *The Hut Six Story: Breaking the Enigma Codes* (M&M Baldwin, 1997)
Wigmore, T; Wilde, F, *Cricket 2.0: Inside the T20 Revolution* (Polaris, 2019)

Articles and reports

Bennett, P, 'Value Of Carbon Offsets Market Has Dropped 61% Since 2022, Report Finds', EcoWatch (31 May 2024), www.ecowatch.com/carbon-offsets-market-value-reliability.html, accessed 5 March 2026
Climate Asset Management, 'Climate Asset Management secures commitments in excess of $1 billion for natural capital projects' (20 September 2024), https://climateassetmanagement.com/insight/climate-asset-management-secures-commitments-in-excess-of-1-billion-for-natural-capital-projects, accessed 5 March 2026
Connell, T, 'Don Macleod: The Land Reform (Scotland) Bill is junk law' SLN (22 October 2025), www.scottishlegal.com/articles/don-macleod-the-land-reform-scotland-bill-is-junk-law, accessed 8 December 2025
Environmental Audit Committee, 'The role of natural capital in the UK's green economy', UK Parliament (2024-2025), https://publications.parliament.uk/pa/cm5901/cmselect/cmenvaud/501/report.html, accessed 5 March 2026
Frontier Insights, 'United Kingdom Voluntary Carbon Offsets and Carbon Neutrality Market Size And Outlook 2033', Verified Market Reports (n.d.), www.verifiedmarketreports.com/frontier-insight/outlook/voluntary-carbon-offsets-and-carbon-neutrality-market/united-kingdom, accessed 5 March 2026
Higgins, B, 'Reform Should Help, Not Punish Landowners', *The Times* (1 April 2025), reproduced at Buccleuch, www.buccleuch.com/benny-higgins-times-column, accessed 5 March 2026
Hive, 'Boothby Wildland', Green Finance Institute (27 October 2025), https://hive.greenfinanceinstitute.com/gfihive/

toolkit/community-engagement/boothby-wildland, accessed 5 March 2026

Investment Stewardship, 'Our approach to engagement on natural capital', BlackRock (n.d.), www.blackrock.com/corporate/literature/publication/blk-commentary-engagement-on-natural-capital.pdf, accessed 5 March 2026

J.P. Morgan Asset Management, 'J.P Morgan Asset Management's Campbell Global Announces Close of $1.5 billion Forest & Climate Solutions Fund II', PR Newswire (8 April 2025), www.prnewswire.com/news-releases/jp-morgan-asset-managements-campbell-global-announces-close-of-1-5-billion-forest--climate-solutions-fund-ii-302423395.html, accessed 5 March 2026

Miltimore, J, 'Charlie Munger's Rules For Life—In His Own Words', Foundation for Economic Education (18 December 2023), https://fee.org/articles/charlie-mungers-rules-for-life-in-his-own-words, accessed 5 March 2026

Nicholles, N, 'Why valuing nature and people is just as important as financials', Reuters (18 March 2025), www.reuters.com/sustainability/sustainable-finance-reporting/why-valuing-nature-people-is-just-important-financials-2025-03-19, accessed 5 March 2026

Oxygen Conservation, 'Oxygen Conservation Carbon Curve' (Summer 2025), www.oxygenconservation.com/news-events/oxygen-conservation-curve-2025, accessed 5 March 2025

Priestley, M, 'Tree planters still outbidding farmers in Scottish uplands', *Farmers Weekly* (20 April 2024), www.fwi.co.uk/business/markets-and-trends/land-markets/tree-planters-still-outbidding-farmers-in-scottish-uplands, accessed 5 March 2026

Tamssom, J and Mauvenu, P, 'AXA IM Alts expands its Natural Capital and Impact investments strategy with new commitments from development finance institutions', AXA IM (10 November 2025), https://alts.axa-im.com/media-centre/axa-im-alts-expands-its-natural-capital-and-impact-investments-strategy-new-commitments-development, accessed 5 March 2026

Thompson, B and Ford, E, 'Climate Asset Management secures commitments in excess of $1 billion for natural capital projects', Climate Asset Management (20 September 2024), https://climateassetmanagement.com/wp-content/uploads/2024/09/Climate-Asset-Management-secures-commitments-of-over-1-billion-for-natural-capital-projects-20.09.24.pdf, accessed 5 March 2026

World Commission on Environment and Development, *Our Common Future* (The Brundtland Report) (Oxford University Press, 1987)

Podcasts

Hughes, D and Humphrey, J, 'Walking away from Mercedes to risk everything for Williams, with F1 Boss James Vowles', *High Performance* (29 January 2024) www.highperformancepodcast.com, 5 March 2026

Courtenay, C, 'The Earl's Evolution of Powderham', *Shoot Room* (15 August 2024), www.youtube.com/watch?v=W-JQQI8HO50, accessed 5 March 2026

Thompson, G, 'Nature Markets Are Broken—Here's How to Fix Them Before It's Too Late', *Shoot Room* (4 September 2025) www.youtube.com/watch?v=aApSZ6fiKWg, accessed 5 March 2026

Miscellaneous

Jay, A; Lynn, J, 'The Moral Dimension', *Yes, Minister* (1982) www.dailymotion.com/video/x5v4ri8, accessed 17 December 2025

Acknowledgements

Every book has a moment when the author sits down to write the acknowledgements and realises, with some alarm, that the list of people who made the thing possible is substantially longer than the list of people who will actually read it. This is that moment.

Rewilding Wealth represents the second act. Not just of Oxygen Conservation as a business, but of a period in my life where everything – the sector, the company, the team, and quite possibly the person writing these words – grew in ways I couldn't have predicted and still don't entirely understand. If *Scaling Conservation* was the story of starting something audacious, this book is the story of what happens when the audacious thing actually starts to look like an underestimation.

None of it – not a single acre, not a single page – would exist without Mark, Lil, Roy, David, Adam, and Tony. These are the people who invested in me in every sense of the word. Not just financially, though that part was fairly important. They invested belief when the evidence was thin, patience when the progress was slower, and trust when I'm sure, on more than one occasion, the rational thing would have been to ask what on earth I thought I was doing. Whenever any of them tells me they're proud of the business, of our culture, of the impact we're having, I go quiet for a moment. Not because I don't know what to say, but because the feeling is too big for whatever I'd say to be adequate. So I'll say it here instead: thank you. For the opportunity of a lifetime.

To Benny, mentor and friend, and one of the few people who can occupy both roles without the second one undermining the first. The best mentors don't just give you advice. They give you permission to trust your own instincts, and then they're honest enough to tell you when your instincts might be wrong. Benny does both, often in the same conversation.

To the entire ExCo, I love that this is your business now too. The fact that we were able to make that possible means the world to me. But it's only the beginning. I suspect the chapters you write in the future will be better than the ones I have.

To Abbey, who took the thoughts rattling around inside my head, many of them half-formed, some of them contradictory, a few of them barely coherent before my third coffee, and organised them into something that resembles a book. That is a more heroic act than it sounds. Anyone who has ever tried to impose structure in this way deserves not just thanks but probably some kind of professional hazard pay.

And then to Helen. Here's the thing about building something like Oxygen Conservation: it requires a particular kind of obsessiveness that is, to put it diplomatically, not always compatible with being a fully functioning human being. Helen is the reason I remain one. Most of the time. None of this happens without her, and the fact that she continues to tolerate me doing it is an act of generosity I try very hard not to take for granted. Thank you for making me a person I don't mind sometimes.

Emma and George, you might read this one day. If you do, I want you to know that this was one of the many reasons I spent so much time at my laptop. I hope you won't mind that. I hope you like some of the ideas. I hope you question more of them. And I hope you improve upon many of the others. That would make all of it worthwhile.

And for the many other people who have been part of our story in ways both profound and fleeting – too many to name, though every one of them deserves to be – thank you. You've made this act an absolute pleasure.

I can't wait for the next one.

The Author

Rich Stockdale is a transformative leader and pioneering environmentalist on a mission to Scale Conservation. Armed with a PhD in data science, he combines relentless commitment with visionary thinking to redefine our relationship with the natural world. He co-founded Oxygen Conservation with Oxygen House Group in 2021 and has rapidly built it into one of the world's most impactful natural capital portfolios, valued at hundreds of millions of pounds and actively transforming over 50,000 acres into thriving ecosystems for people and wildlife.

Rich is determined to make natural capital a mainstream asset class. With the ambitious target of managing over £1 billion in assets by 2030, he is reshaping how the world values nature and creating positive impact on an incredible scale.

- www.oxygenconservation.com
- www.linkedin.com/in/richstockdale

www.ingramcontent.com/pod-product-compliance
Lightning Source LLC
LaVergne TN
LVHW040517210926
848480LV00007BA/1490
* 9 7 8 1 7 8 1 3 3 9 7 7 0 *